Academic
Learning
Series

Microsoft®
Windows® 2000
Professional

Lab Manual

Microsoft®

PUBLISHED BY
Microsoft Press
A Division of Microsoft Corporation
One Microsoft Way
Redmond, Washington 98052-6399

Library of Congress Cataloging-in-Publication Data
MCSE Training Kit--Microsoft Windows 2000 Professional / Microsoft Corporation.
    p. cm.
  Includes index.
    ISBN 1-57231-901-1
    ISBN 0-7356-1048-7 (Academic Learning Series)
    1. Electronic data processing personnel--Certification. 2. Microsoft
software--Examinations--Study guides. 3. Microsoft Windows (Computer file) I.
Microsoft Corporation.

  QA76.3.M33454 2000
  005.4'4769--dc21   99-059499

Printed and bound in the United States of America.

1 2 3 4 5 6 7 8 9   WCWC   5 4 3 2 1 0

Distributed in Canada by Penguin Books Canada Limited.

A CIP catalogue record for this book is available from the British Library.

Microsoft Press books are available through booksellers and distributors worldwide. For further information about international editions, contact your local Microsoft Corporation office or contact Microsoft Press International directly at fax (425) 936-7329. Visit our Web site at mspress.microsoft.com. Send comments to *tkinput@microsoft.com*.

Acquisitions Editor: Thomas Pohlmann
Project Editor: Julie Miller
Technical Editor: L. J. Locher
Manuscript Editor: Linda Robinson

Author: Rick Wallace

Part No. 097-0003106

Introduction

This Lab Manual supplements the *ALS: Microsoft Windows 2000 Professional* textbook. The lab exercises in this manual are designed to be performed in a classroom by a group of students under the supervision of an instructor. This is in contrast to the hands-on practice exercises in the textbook, which are designed to be performed by individual students on computers separate from the classroom. The lab exercises in this manual and the hands-on practice exercises in the textbook form an essential part of your training because it is difficult to truly understand and use the operating system and its features without having first had the opportunity to explore the menus, options, and responses.

The labs in this manual do not precisely mirror the exercises in the textbook. The Lab Manual exercises are written for a domain environment, while the textbook practice exercises are designed to be performed on stand-alone computers. The computer names, IP addresses, most shared resources, and other specific references in this Lab Manual are different than those in the textbook. Also, because it is not possible to predict each institution's local networking requirements, there might be slight differences between the names and addresses in your classroom and those appearing in these lab exercises. Your instructor will explain any differences.

The labs are performed in a classroom that is set up as an isolated network. The instructor computer, Instructor*x* (where *x* is replaced by a number) is a Microsoft Windows 2000 domain controller. The instructor computer includes shared folders that support the lab exercises.

The old saying "The way to get to Carnegie Hall is to practice, practice, practice" is equally true of the pursuit of competence as you prepare for the Microsoft certification tests. The Microsoft Certified Professional (MCP) exams are demanding. One of the best ways to become confident in the use of Windows 2000 Professional is to complete all the assigned lab exercises in this manual as well as the hands-on exercises in the textbook.

Lab Navigation

The lab exercises in this manual and the practice exercises in the textbook use drop-down menus to demonstrate how to navigate through Windows interface elements, such as Microsoft Management Console (MMC). There are rare instances when drop-down menus are not available, and in these cases, explicit instructions are provided for using context menus. You can activate an object's context menu by right-clicking the object.

The lab exercises and textbook practice exercises use the Windows default double-click setting: double-click to open an item (single-click to select). Do not configure the computers to use the optional single-click to open an item (point to select) setting.

Lab 1: Installing Microsoft Windows 2000 Professional

Objectives

After completing this lab, you will be able to

- Install Windows 2000 Professional by connecting to a network share.
- Log on locally to a computer running Windows 2000 Professional.
- Join your computer to a domain.
- Log on to a domain.

Estimated time to complete this lab: 50 minutes

Exercise 1
Installing Windows 2000 Professional over the Network

In this exercise, you install Windows 2000 Professional by using a legacy version of a Microsoft Windows operating system and connecting to a network share on the instructor's computer to perform an over-the-network installation. The following steps are based on a computer running Windows NT Workstation 4.0. The steps for other legacy versions of Windows operating systems can vary slightly.

▶ **To install Windows 2000 Professional**

1. Power on your computer, and log on locally as Administrator using a password of "password".

2. Click the Start button, and then click Run.

   A Run dialog box appears.

3. In the Open combo box, type **\\instructor*x*\w2000pro** (where *x* is the instructor number obtained from your instructor) and then click OK.

   An Enter Network Password dialog box appears because you are not logged on to the domain and cannot access other resources on the domain.

4. In the Connect As text box, type **Student*z*** (where *z* is your student ID number), and in the Password text box, type **password**. Click OK.

   A window appears showing the folders in the w2000pro share.

5. Double-click the \I386 folder.

   A window appears listing the files in the I386 folder.

6. Scroll through the listed files, and locate Winnt32.

7. Double-click Winnt32.

   A Windows 2000 Setup wizard appears. Notice that in addition to the initial installation of Windows 2000 Professional, you can use Windows 2000 Setup to upgrade the current installation to Windows 2000 Professional.

8. Select the Install A New Copy Of Windows 2000 (Clean Install) radio button, and then click Next.

   The Windows 2000 Licensing Agreement page appears.

9. Read the Licensing Agreement, select the I Accept This Agreement radio button, and then click Next to agree with the licensing terms.

   The Your Product Key page appears.

10. Enter the product key provided by your instructor, and then click Next.

    The Select Special Options page appears, which provides you with a way to customize Windows 2000 Professional for different languages, installation, and accessibility options.

11. Click the Advanced Options button.

    The Advanced Options dialog box appears, which allows you to change the location of Windows 2000 files that you are using to install Windows 2000 Professional on this computer, and to change the name and location of the Windows 2000 installation folder.

12. Click Cancel to return to the Special Options page.

13. Click Next to continue with the installation.

    The Upgrading To The Windows 2000 NTFS File System page appears.

14. Read the information contained on the Upgrading To The Windows 2000 NTFS File System page.

15. Ensure that the Yes, Upgrade My Drive radio button is selected, and then click Next.

    A Please Wait page appears briefly, and then a Copying Installation Files page appears, which displays a progress indicator showing the files Setup is copying. Notice that the page indicates that if you are installing using a CD-ROM, the file copying should take only a few minutes, but if you are installing files over a network, the copying of files can take longer, depending on network conditions.

    When the copying files portion of Setup concludes, the computer reboots and the Welcome To Setup screen appears. Notice that in addition to the initial installation of Windows 2000 Professional, you can use Windows 2000 Setup to repair a damaged Windows 2000 installation.

Note At this point in the installation, if you want to quit Setup for any reason, you can press F3 to exit.

---

16. Read the Welcome To Setup screen, and press ENTER to continue.

    Setup lists the existing partitions and unpartitioned space on the computer.

Note If you are using a dual-boot computer, your instructor may want you to install Windows 2000 Professional to a partition other than C. To delete an existing partition, select the partition and press D. Follow the directions on the screen to complete the deletion. To create a new partition in the unpartitioned space, select the unpartitioned space and press C. Follow the directions on the screen to finish creating the new partition. You should create *only* the partition to hold the Windows 2000 Professional installation. Any other partitions should be created using Disk Manager after the installation is completed.

---

17. Press ENTER to select the default C: partition as the location for the Windows 2000 Professional installation.

    Setup prompts you that Windows 2000 recognizes the partition you selected, but that another operating system is installed on the partition.

18. Press C to continue using the selected C: partition for the installation.

    Setup prompts you to select the file system you want to use to format the partition. You can choose either the NTFS file system or the FAT file system. There are only two cases where you would not choose NTFS:

    - **Dual booting**. You are installing Windows 2000 Professional on a computer that has an operating system loaded which cannot use NTFS, and you must keep that operating system installed. When you start your computer, you have the ability to *dual boot*—in other words, boot either of the two operating systems.

    - **Down-level clients**. You have computers in your network that must access files on the computer you are installing and those client computers cannot use NTFS.

    In all other cases, you would choose NTFS because it provides many new features, including file-level and folder-level security, disk compression, disk quotas, and file encryption.

Note When you no longer need to dual-boot or to support down-level clients, you can switch to NTFS. However, if you reformat the partition, you erase all the information on that partition and you have to reinstall Windows 2000 Professional. Windows 2000 Professional therefore provides the Convert command. You can use this command to convert a partition to NTFS without reformatting the partition and losing all the information it contains.

The syntax of the command is as follows: convert volume /FS:NTFS

To convert the C partition to NTFS, you would open a command prompt, type **convert C /FS:NTFS**, and then press ENTER.

---

19. Press C to convert the drive to NTFS.

    Setup informs you that it has detected one or more older versions of Windows NT on this computer and informs you that these versions will not start unless they are upgraded to Windows NT 4.0 with Service Pack 4 or greater before you install Windows 2000. You can press C to continue or F3 to quit Setup.

20. Press C to continue.

    Setup examines the partition and then copies files to the default Windows 2000 Professional installation folders. This might take several minutes.

    When the MS-DOS portion of the installation is complete, Setup reboots the computer and converts the partition to NTFS.

    Once the computer has rebooted, Setup configures the NTFS folder and file permissions for the operating system files, detects the hardware devices in the computer, and then installs and configures device drivers to support all the detected hardware. This process will take several minutes.

The Regional Settings page appears. The Regional Settings page provides you with a way to customize Windows 2000 Professional for different regions, languages, and keyboard layouts.

21. Next to the To Change System Or User Locale Settings, Click Customize option, click the Customize button.

    What is the default locale?

    _____

    In the English (United States) locale, how do you set your clock to be a 24-hour clock instead of a 12-hour clock? (If you are unfamiliar with a 24-hour clock, here are a few samples of how a 24-hour clock expresses time: one o'clock in the afternoon is 13:00, three o'clock in the afternoon is 15:00, and midnight is 24:00.)

    _____

    _____

22. Click Cancel to clear any changes you have made to the locale or language settings and to close the Regional Options page.

Note You can modify regional settings after you install Windows 2000 Professional by using Regional Options in Control Panel. For more information, see Chapter 4 in the *ALS: Microsoft Windows 2000 Professional* textbook, "Using Windows Control Panel."

23. On the Regional Settings page, click Next to continue with the installation.

    The Personalize Your Software page appears, prompting you for your name and organization name.

Note Setup uses your organization name to generate the default computer name. Many applications that you install later will use this information for product registration and document identification.

24. In the Name text box, type your name, and in the Organization text box, type the name of your organization. Click Next.

    The Computer Name And Administrator Password page appears. Notice that Setup has suggested a computer name based on your organization name.

25. In the Computer Name text box, type **Computerz**, where *z* is the student number assigned to you by your instructor.

    Notice that Windows 2000 displays the computer name in all capital letters, no matter how you type it. The computer name can have a maximum of 15 characters and must be unique on the network.

26. In the Administrator Password and Confirm Password text boxes, type **password** and then click Next.

Important For the labs in this course, you will use "password" for the Administrator account. In a real-world situation, you would always use a complex password for the Administrator account (one that others cannot easily guess). Microsoft recommends mixing numbers, symbols, and uppercase and lowercase letters (for example, Wp5*u8).

If a modem is connected to the computer on which you are installing Windows 2000 Professional, the Modem Dialing Information page appears. Otherwise, Setup displays the Date And Time Settings page. If your computer doesn't have a modem, go to step 31.

27. In the What Country/Region Are You In Now? drop-down box, ensure the correct country/region is selected.

28. In the What Area Code (Or City Code) Are You In Now? text box, type in the correct area code or city code.

29. If you must dial a number to get an outside line, in the If You Dial A Number To Get An Outside Line, What Is It? text box, type in the correct number.

30. Ensure that the correct phone system is selected under The Phone System At This Location Uses:, and then click Next.

The Date And Time Settings page appears.

31. On the Date And Time Settings page, ensure that the Date & Time setting and the Time Zone setting are correct for your location.

32. If you want Windows 2000 Professional to automatically change the time on your computer for daylight savings time changes, ensure that the Automatically Adjust Clock For Daylight Savings Changes check box is selected and then click Next.

Note If you have configured your computer for dual booting with another operating system that can also adjust your clock for daylight savings time changes, enable this feature for only the operating system you use most frequently so that the daylight savings adjustment will occur only once.

Setup displays the Network Settings progress indicator and automatically installs network software so that you can connect to other networks and to the Internet. This will take a few moments. After the files are copied, the Setup program prompts you to choose whether to use typical or custom settings for configuring network components.

33. Select the Custom Settings radio button, and then click Next.

    The Networking Components page appears. Notice that there are three components installed by default:

    - **Client For Microsoft Networks.** This component allows you to access file and print shares located on other computers running a Microsoft Windows operating system.

    - **File And Printer Sharing For Microsoft Networks.** This component allows you to share your own computer resources.

    - **Internet Protocol (TCP/IP).** This component is an industry-standard suite of protocols that provides communications across networks of computers with various hardware, architectures, and operating systems.

34. Click the Install button.

    The Select Network Component Type dialog box appears. Notice that you can install other clients, services, and protocols.

35. Click Cancel to return to the Network Components page, and then click Next.

    The Workgroup Or Computer Domain page appears. Notice that there are two options:

    - No, This Computer Is Not On A Network, Or Is On A Network Without A Domain. This is the default selection.

    - Yes, Make This Computer A Member Of The Following Domain.

Note Normally when you install Windows 2000 Professional on a computer, you would join a domain at this point of the installation. For purposes of this class, you will not join the domain until after the Windows 2000 Professional installation is complete.

---

36. Ensure that the default option No, This Computer Is Not On A Network, Or Is On A Network Without A Domain is selected, and in the Workgroup Or Computer Domain text box, ensure that it says WORKGROUP.

37. Click Next.

    The Installing Components page appears, displaying a progress indicator as Setup copies files to install and configure Windows 2000 Professional components. This process will take several minutes.

    The Performing Final Tasks page then appears and displays a progress indicator as Setup installs Start menu items, registers components, saves settings, and removes any temporary files. This process will take several minutes.

    The Completing The Windows 2000 Setup Wizard page appears.

38. Click the Finish button to continue setting up Windows 2000 Professional.

    The computer restarts, and the Network Identification wizard appears.

► **To configure your network**

1. To use the Network Identification wizard, click Next on the Welcome To The Network Identification Wizard page.

Note If you had joined this computer to a domain during the installation, the User Account dialog box would appear, allowing you to add a user account to the local security database of the computer. A user account that you add to the local security database must be an existing network account—one that currently exists in the domain security database.

The Users Of This Computer page appears. Notice that there are two options:

- Users Must Enter A User Name And Password To Use This Computer.
- Windows Always Assumes The Following User Has Logged On To This Computer.

2. Select the Users Must Enter A User Name And Password To Use This Computer radio button, and then click Next.

The Completing The Network Identification Wizard page appears.

3. Click the Finish button.

The Windows 2000 Professional installation is now complete, and your computer is a member of the default workgroup named Workgroup. The Log On To Windows dialog box appears, and you may now log on to the local computer.

Exercise 2
Logging On Locally to a Computer

In this exercise, you log on locally to a computer running Windows 2000 Professional. You will review the selections on the Programs menu and then configure your computer so that the Administrative Tools menu appears on the Programs menu for the Administrator.

► **To log on locally to the computer**

1. In the User Name text box, ensure that it says Administrator, and in the Password text box, type **password** and then click OK.

   You have now logged on to the local computer as Administrator. The Getting Started With Windows 2000 dialog box appears.

2. Clear the Show This Screen At Startup check box, and then click the Exit button to close the Getting Started With Windows 2000 dialog box.

3. Click the Start button, and then click Programs.

   What selections are listed on the Programs menu?

   _____

4. Click the Desktop to close the Programs menu.

► **To add the Administrative Tools menu to the Programs menu**

1. Right-click the Taskbar, and then click Properties.

   The Taskbar And Start Menu Properties dialog box appears.

2. Click the Advanced tab.

3. In the Start Menu Settings list box, select Display Administrative Tools. There should now be a check mark in the check box in front of Display Administrative Tools.

4. Click OK to apply your changes and to close the Taskbar And Start Menu Properties dialog box.

5. Click the Start button, click Programs, verify that Administrative Tools is now listed on the Programs menu, and then click the Desktop to close the Programs menu.

Exercise 3
Joining the Corpy Domain

In this exercise, you join your computer to the Corpy domain.

▶   **To join a domain**

1. Right-click My Computer, and then click Properties.

   The System Properties dialog box appears, with the General tab active.

2. Click the Network Identification tab.

   Notice the option, To Rename This Computer Or Join A Domain, Click Properties.

3. Click the Properties button.

   The Identification Changes dialog box appears.

4. In the Member Of group box, click the Domain radio button, and then in the Domain text box, type **Corpy** (where *y* is the number your instructor has assigned to your domain) and then click OK.

   The Domain User Name And Password dialog box appears.

5. In the Name text box, type **Studentz** (where *z* is your student number), and in the Password text box, type **password**.

Note Your Studentz logon worked because during classroom setup your instructor allowed Studentz to add computers to the corpy.corp.com domain.

---

6. Click OK.

   A Network Identification message box appears, welcoming you to the Corpy domain.

7. Click OK to close the message box.

   A Network Identification message box appears, informing you that you must reboot your computer for the changes to take place.

8. Click OK to close the message box.

9. Click OK to close the System Properties dialog box.

   A System Settings Change message box appears, asking you if you want to reboot the computer now.

10. Click the Yes button to restart your computer.

Note Your computer is now a member of the corpy.corp.com domain.

Exercise 4
Logging On to the Corpy Domain

In this exercise, you log on to the Corpy domain. You will also review the selections on the Programs menu and then configure your computer so that the Administrative Tools menu appears on the Programs menu for Studentz.

► **To log on to the domain**

1. Press CTRL+ALT+DELETE.

   The Log On To Windows dialog box appears.

2. In the Log On To Windows dialog box, click the Options button.

   A Log On To drop-down list appears.

3. In the User Name text box, type **Studentz** (where z is your student number), and in the Password text box, type **password**.

   Notice the Log On Using Dial-up Connection check box. This check box enables a user to connect to a domain server by using dial-up networking. There is also a Shutdown button that allows you to shut down the computer.

4. Click the down arrow at the end of the Log On To drop-down list.

   What are the available selections in the Log On To box?

   _____

   _____

5. In the Log On To drop-down list, select Corpy and then click OK.

   The Getting Started With Windows 2000 dialog box appears.

   In Exercise 2, step 2, you cleared the Show This Screen At Startup check box and then exited the Getting Started With Windows 2000 dialog box. Why did the Getting Started With Windows 2000 dialog box appear again?

   _____

   _____

   _____

   _____

   _____

6. Clear the Show This Screen At Startup check box, and exit the Getting Started With Windows 2000 dialog box.

7. Review the selections on the Programs menu, and then configure your computer so that the Administrative Tools menu appears on the Programs menu for Studentz. (If you have forgotten how to configure your computer so that the Administrative Tools menu appears on the Programs menu, see Exercise 2.)

Lab 2: Creating a Customized Console with Microsoft Management Console

Objectives

After completing this lab, you will be able to

- Create a custom console for local administration.
- Modify an existing console and create a custom console for remote administration.
- Use a custom console to administer the local computer.
- Use a custom console to administer a remote computer.

Estimated time to complete this lab: 30 minutes

Exercise 1
Creating Customized Consoles

In this exercise, you will create a customized Microsoft Management Console (MMC) console containing the Removable Storage Management snap-in and you will point the snap-in to the local computer for local administration.

▶   **To create a customized console**

1. Log on locally to your computer as Administrator with a password of "password".

Note Make sure you log on locally to your computer, Computer*z* (where *z* is your student number), and not to the domain.

---

2. Click the Start button, click Run, in the Open combo box type **mmc**, and then click OK.

   MMC starts and displays an empty console.

3. Maximize the Console1 window and the Console Root window.

Note To maximize a window, click its Maximize button located in the upper right-hand corner of the window.

---

4. To view the currently configured options, click Options on the Console menu.

   Notice that the default console mode is Author mode and that the Description explains that Author mode grants users full access to all MMC functionality—including the ability to add or remove snap-ins, create new windows, create taskpad views and tasks, and view all portions of the console tree.

5. Click the down arrow at the end of the Console Mode drop-down list.

   What other modes are available?

   _____

   _____

   _____

6. In the Console Mode drop-down list, make sure that Author Mode is selected and then click OK.

7. On the Console menu, click Add/Remove Snap-In.

   The Add/Remove Snap-In dialog box appears.

8. Click the Add button.

   The Add Standalone Snap-In dialog box appears.

   Notice the available snap-ins. MMC allows you to add one or more snap-ins to a console, enabling you to create your own customized management tools.

9. Select Removable Storage Management, and then click the Add button.

   The Select Computer dialog box appears. Notice that you can specify the computer you want this snap-in to manage.

10. Make sure that Local Computer: (The Computer This Console Is Running On) is selected, and then click the Finish button.

11. Close the Add Standalone Snap-In dialog box.

   Notice that Removable Storage (Local) appears in the Add/Remove Snap-In dialog box.

12. Click OK to close the Add/Remove Snap-In dialog box.

13. On the Console menu, click Save As.

14. In the File Name text box, type **RSM** and then click the Save button.

   The name of your console appears on the MMC title bar.

15. On the Console menu, click Exit.

   You have now created and saved a customized console named RSM for use on your local computer.

Exercise 2
Creating a Remote Administration Console

In this exercise, you will modify an existing custom console by adding the Removable Storage Management snap-in to it and point the snap-in at your partner's computer so that you can perform remote administration.

▶ **To add snap-ins to a console**

1. Click the Start button, click Run, in the Open combo box type **mmc**, and then click OK.

2. On the Console menu, click Open.

    MMC displays the Open dialog box. Notice that the console you created in Exercise 1 (RSM.msc) was saved in the Administrative Tools folder.

    What is the full path to RSM.msc?

    _____

    _____

3. Click RSM, and then click Open.

    Microsoft Windows 2000 opens the RSM console that you saved previously.

4. On the Console menu, click Add/Remove Snap-In.

    The Add/Remove Snap-In dialog box appears, with the Standalone tab active. Notice that Removable Storage (Local) is the only loaded snap-in. You will add a snap-in to the console root.

5. In the Add/Remove Snap-In dialog box, click the Add button.

    The Add Standalone Snap-In dialog box appears.

6. In the Add Standalone Snap-In dialog box, select Removable Storage Management and then click the Add button.

    The Select Computer dialog box appears, allowing you to specify whether you want to administer the local computer or another computer in the domain.

7. Select Another Computer, and then click the Browse button in order to select another computer on the domain.

    The Enter Network Password dialog box appears.

    Why does the Enter Network Password dialog box appear? (Hint: Who are you logged on as?)

    _____

    _____

    _____

    _____

8. In the Connect As text box, type **Student**z (where z is your student number), in the Password and Confirm Password text boxes, type **password**, and then click OK.

   The Select Computer dialog box appears.

   Note You are now logged on to the domain. The Select Computer dialog box lists all of the computers in the Corpy domain, allowing you to choose a remote computer to administer. Ask your partner for the name of his/her computer.

9. In the Name list box, select Computerp (your partner's computer) and then click OK.

   When you click OK, the current Select Computer dialog box listing the computers in your domain is closed. The Select Computer dialog box that gives you the option of selecting either the local computer or another computer reappears. Computerp is listed in the Another Computer text box.

10. Click the Finish button.

11. Close the Add Standalone Snap-In dialog box.

12. Click OK to close the Add/Remove Snap-In dialog box.

    Notice that both Removable Storage (Local)—which allows you to use Removable Storage Management on your own computer—and Removable Storage (Computerp)—which allows you to use Removable Storage Management for remote administration on your partner's computer—now appear in the console tree.

    Tip To see the entire folder name, drag the border between the Console pane and the Details pane to the right.

Exercise 3
Using a Custom Console

In this exercise, you will use the RSM custom console you created in Exercise 1 for local administration to determine the removable storage devices on your computer.

▶   **To determine the removable storage devices on your computer**

1. In the console tree of the RSM console, expand the Removable Storage (Local) folder and then expand Physical Locations.

   What type of removable storage devices are on your computer?

   _____

2. On the Console menu, click Exit to close the RSM console.

   A MMC dialog box appears, asking whether you want to save the console settings.

3. Click the Yes button.

Exercise 4
Using a Custom Console for Remote Administration

In this exercise, you will use the RSM custom console you created in Exercise 2 for remote administration to determine the removable storage devices on a remote computer.

▶ **To determine the removable storage devices on a remote computer**

1. Log on to the domain as Student*z* (where *z* is your student number) with a password of "password".

2. Click the Start button, click Run, type **mmc**, and then click OK.

3. On the Console menu, click Open.

   What custom consoles are listed? Why?

   _____

   _____

   _____

   _____

4. Click Cancel to close the Open dialog box.

5. Use Windows Explorer to copy the RSM custom console from C:\Documents and Settings\Administrator\Start Menu\Programs\Administrative Tools to C:\Documents and Settings \Student*z*\Start Menu\Programs\Administrative Tools.

6. Close Windows Explorer.

7. On the Console menu, click Open.

   The Open dialog box appears with RSM listed.

Note Custom consoles appear in the user tree under C:\Documents and Settings for the user who created them. One way to distribute a custom console is to copy it to another user's user tree under C:\Documents and Settings. You could also create a share containing all custom consoles.

---

8. Select RSM, and then click Open.

   MMC opens the RSM custom console.

9. Maximize both the RSM window and the Console Root window.

10. In the console tree, expand the Removable Storage (Computer*p*) folder (your partner's computer) and then expand Physical Locations.

    What types of removable storage devices are on your partner's computer?

    _____

    Close all open windows and log off.

Lab 3: Using Task Scheduler

Objectives

After completing this lab, you will be able to

- Use Task Scheduler to schedule tasks.
- Configure the Task Scheduler advanced options.

Estimated time to complete this lab: 20 minutes

Exercise 1
Using Task Scheduler to Schedule Tasks

In this exercise, you will configure Task Scheduler to automatically start a task at a predetermined time.

▶ **To schedule a task to start automatically**

1. Log on to your local computer as Administrator with a password of "password".

2. Click the Start button, point to Settings, click Control Panel, and then double-click Scheduled Tasks.

   Windows 2000 Professional opens the Scheduled Tasks window. Because no tasks are currently scheduled, only the Add Scheduled Task icon appears.

3. Double-click the Add Scheduled Task icon.

   The Scheduled Task Wizard page appears.

4. Click Next.

   A list of currently installed programs appears. To schedule a program that isn't registered with Windows 2000, use the Browse button to locate the program.

5. Select Solitaire, and then click Next.

   Notice that Solitaire is the name assigned to the task by default.

6. Under Perform This Task, select the When I Log On radio button, and then click Next.

Note The wizard requires you to enter the name and password of a user account. When Task Scheduler runs the scheduled task, the program receives all of the rights and permissions of the user account that you enter here. The program is also bound by any restrictions on the user account. Notice that the name of the user currently logged on is already filled in as the default. You must type the correct password for the user account in both password boxes before you can continue.

7. In both the Password and the Confirm Password text boxes, type **password**.

8. Click Next.

Note Notice the Open The Advanced Properties For This Task When I Click Finish check box. Advanced Properties allows you to schedule a task to run at a set time of day or on a specific schedule.

9. Click the Finish button.

   Notice that the wizard added the task to the list of scheduled tasks.

10. To confirm that you scheduled the task successfully, log off and then log on to your local computer as Administrator with a password of "password".

    Notice that Solitaire automatically started when you logged on.

11. Play one game of Solitaire and whether you win or lose the game, close Solitaire.

Exercise 2
Configuring the Task Scheduler Advanced Options

In this exercise, you will review the Task Scheduler advanced options. You will then use the Task Scheduler advanced options to open Solitaire every day for one week at a specified time.

▶ **To configure Task Scheduler advanced options**

1. In the Scheduled Tasks window, double-click the Solitaire icon.

   The Solitaire dialog box appears, with the Task tab active.

2. Click the Schedule tab.

3. Under Scheduled Task, select Weekly.

4. Under Start Time, set the time for 4 minutes from the current system time.

5. Ensure that the Every spin box is set to the default of one Week and in the On: group box select every day of the week.

   To confirm that you scheduled the task successfully, wait for the time that you set in step 4 of this procedure. Solitaire will start.

6. Close Solitaire.

7. Close the Scheduled Tasks window.

8. Log off your computer.

Lab 4: Using Control Panel to Change Operating System Settings

Objectives

After completing this lab, you will be able to use Control Panel to

- Set the screen resolution and font size.
- Calculate the amount of RAM installed on your computer.
- Configure accessibility options.
- Configure startup and recovery options.

Estimated time to complete this lab: 25 minutes

Exercise 1
Using Control Panel to Configure Screen Resolution and Font Size

In this exercise, you will use the Display Properties dialog box to configure screen resolution and font size.

▶   **To configure screen resolution and font size**

1. Log on locally to Computerz as Administrator with a password of "password".

2. Click the Start button, point to Settings, and then click Control Panel.

3. In Control Panel, double-click the Display icon.

   The Display Properties dialog box appears, with the Background tab active.

4. Click the Settings tab.

   What are your current settings for Colors and Screen Area?

   _____

   _____

   What is the range of values available for Screen Area on your computer? (Drag the Screen Area slider to vary the screen resolution.)

   _____

5. Drag the Screen Area slider to the greatest number of pixels allowable for your hardware.

6. Click OK.

   A Display Properties message box appears, indicating that Microsoft Windows will now apply your new desktop settings.

7. Click OK to close the Display Properties message box.

   A Monitor Settings message box appears, indicating that your desktop has been reconfigured and asking if you would like to keep these settings.

Note If you do not respond in 15 seconds, the settings will revert to your original settings.

8. If you like the new settings, click the Yes button. If you don't like the new settings, click No.

   If the new settings are too small to read, wait for 15 seconds and they will revert to the original settings.

   From your observations, fill in the following blank: The higher the number of pixels, the _____ information you can display on your screen.

   _____

9. Click the Advanced button.

   The Monitor and Adapter Type Properties dialog box appears, with the General tab active. Notice that you can change your font selection. What is your current font size?

   _____

10. In the Font Size drop-down list, select Large Fonts and then click the Apply button.

    A Change System Font message box appears indicating that changes in the system font will take effect after the fonts have been installed and Windows 2000 has been restarted.

11. Click OK.

    If this is the first time you are using large fonts, a Change System Font message box appears asking if you are sure you want to change the system font size and install new fonts. If this isn't the first time you've used large fonts, skip to step 13.

12. Click the Yes button to install new fonts.

    A General dialog box appears informing you that the required files are already installed on your computer and asking if you would like to use the existing installed fonts.

13. Click the Yes button to use the installed fonts.

14. On the Display Properties dialog box, click the Apply button.

    A System Settings Change message box appears, indicating that you must restart your computer before the new settings will take effect and asking if you would like to restart your computer now.

15. Click the Yes button to restart your computer.

    Adjusting the font size allows you to increase the pixel count and still easily read the text on the display.

Exercise 2
Calculating the Amount of RAM Installed on Your Computer

Normally you use the amount of RAM installed on your computer to calculate the recommended paging file size for your computer. In this exercise, you are going to look up the recommended paging file size and calculate the amount of RAM installed on your computer.

▶ **To calculate the amount of RAM**

1. Log on locally to Computerz as Administrator with a password of "password".

   How do you calculate the recommended paging file size?

   _____

   _____

   _____

2. Click the Start button, point to Settings, and then click Control Panel.

3. In Control Panel, double-click the System icon.

   The System Properties dialog box appears, with the General tab active.

4. Select the Advanced tab, and click the Performance Options button.

   The Performance Options dialog box appears. Notice the Virtual Memory setting.

5. Click the Change button.

   The Virtual Memory dialog box appears. Notice that the Total Paging File Size For All Drives lists the following values: the Minimum Allowed, the Recommended, and the Currently Allocated.

Note Normally you could use the amount of RAM in your computer to calculate the recommended paging file size. On your classroom computer, you probably don't know the amount of RAM installed, but you do know the recommended paging file size.

Based on the recommended paging file size, what is the amount of RAM installed on your computer?

_____

_____

_____

If you wanted to change the initial size of your paging file, you would increase or decrease the value in the Initial Size (MB:) text box and then click the Set button. If you wanted to change the maximum size that your paging file can expand to, you would increase or decrease the value in the Maximum Size (MB:) text box and then click the Set button.

6. Click Cancel to close the Virtual Memory dialog box.

7. Click Cancel to close the Performance Options dialog box.

8. Click Cancel to close the System Properties dialog box.

   Leave the Control Panel open. You will use it in the next exercise.

Exercise 3
Using Control Panel to Configure Accessibility Options

In this exercise, you are going to use Control Panel to configure StickyKeys on your computer.

► **To configure keyboard options**

1. In Control Panel, double-click the Accessibility Options icon.

   The Accessibility Options dialog box appears, with the Keyboard tab active.

   What are the three Keyboard accessibility options?

   _____

2. Select the Use StickyKeys check box, and then click the Settings button.

   The Settings for StickyKeys dialog box appears.

   In the Keyboard Shortcut group box, it states that the shortcut key for StickyKeys is Press The <Shift> Key Five Times.

   In the Options group box, there are two options: Press Modifier Key Twice To Lock and Turn StickyKeys Off If Two Keys Are Pressed At Once. Both of these options are selected by default.

   In the Notification group box, there are also two options: Make Sounds When Modifier Key Is Pressed and Show StickyKeys Status On Screen. Both of these options are selected by default.

3. Click OK to close the Settings For StickyKeys dialog box.

4. Click the Apply button, and then click OK to close the Accessibility Options dialog box.

5. Close Control Panel.

6. Press CTRL.

   You should hear a sound indicating that StickyKeys is turned on.

7. Press ALT, and then press DELETE.

   You should hear a sound after each keystroke indicating that StickyKeys is turned on.

   The Windows Security dialog box appears, indicating that StickyKeys is turned on.

8. Click Cancel to close the Windows Security dialog box.

9. Press CTRL+ALT.

   You should hear a sound indicating that StickyKeys is turned off. Why is StickyKeys turned off?

   _____

   _____

   _____

10. Click the Start button, point to Settings, and then click Control Panel.

11. In Control Panel, double-click the Accessibility Options icon.

    The Accessibility Options dialog box appears, with the Keyboard tab active.

12. Click the Display tab.

    The Display tab is brought to the front. Notice you can select the Use High Contrast check box. If you select Use High Contrast, Windows 2000 uses colors and fonts designed for easy reading.

13. Select the Use High Contrast check box, and then click the Settings button.

    The Settings For High Contrast dialog box appears. Notice that the shortcut key is Left Alt + Left Shift + Print Screen.

14. In the High Contrast Color Scheme group box, select the Custom radio button.

15. Click the down arrow to activate the Custom drop-down list, select High Contrast #1 (Large), and click OK.

16. Click the Apply button, and then click OK to close the Accessibility Options dialog box.

17. Press LEFT ALT + LEFT SHIFT + PRINT SCREEN to turn off High Contrast.

18. Close all open dialog boxes, but leave Control Panel open.

Exercise 4
Using Control Panel to Configure Startup and Recovery Options

In this exercise, you will use the System Properties dialog box to configure startup and recovery options.

▶ **To configure startup and recovery options**

1. In Control Panel, double-click the System icon.

2. On the Advanced tab of the System Properties dialog box, click the Startup And Recovery button.

   The Startup And Recovery dialog box appears.

3. Under System Startup, change the number of seconds that the operating system list is displayed from 30 seconds to 15 seconds.

   Will changing this time make a difference on your computer? Why or why not?

   _____

   _____

   _____

   _____

4. Review the System Failure group box selections.

   If you were going to configure your computer to respond to a System Failure, what options would you configure? Why did you make those selections?

   _____

   _____

   _____

   _____

   _____

   _____

5. Click OK to close the Startup And Recovery dialog box.

   If you made any changes to the settings in the System Failure group box, a System Control Panel Applet message box appears, indicating that the changes you made require you to restart your computer before the changes can take effect.

6. If the System Control Panel Applet message box appears, click OK to close it and then click OK to close the System Properties dialog box.

7. If a System Settings Change message box appears, asking if you want to restart your computer now, click the Yes button.

   If you have more than one selection on your operating system list when the computer reboots, you will notice that the counter for the number of seconds the list is displayed now starts at 15 seconds.

Lab 5: Using the Registry Editor

Objectives

After completing this lab, you will be able to

- Use the Registry Editor, Regedt32.exe, to view the registry.
- Use the Registry Editor's Find Key command.
- Use the Registry Editor to view the registry on a remote computer.

Estimated time to complete this lab: 20 minutes

Exercise 1
Viewing Information in the Registry

In this exercise, you will use the Registry Editor to view information in the registry. You will determine information such as the date of the System BIOS, the processor on your computer, and the version of the operating system.

▶   **To view information in the registry**

1. Log on locally to Computerz as Administrator with a password of "password".

2. Click the Start button, and then click Run.

3. In the Open combo box, type **regedt32** and then click OK.

   The Registry Editor starts.

4. On the Options menu, click Read Only Mode to place a check mark to the left of that option in the drop-down list.

5. On the View menu, ensure that the Tree And Data option is selected. This option is selected when a check mark is displayed in front of it in the drop-down list.

6. Maximize the Registry Editor window, and then maximize the HKEY_LOCAL_MACHINE On Local Machine window.

7. Double-click the HARDWARE\RESOURCEMAP\Hardware Abstraction Layer subkey to expand it.

   What Hardware Abstraction Layer (HAL) is installed?

   _____

8. Double-click the HARDWARE\DESCRIPTION\SYSTEM\CentralProcessor subkey to expand it.

9. Under Central Processor, click 0.

   What is the VendorIdentifier for your central processor?

   _____

   According to the Identifier for your central processor, what type of processor is installed in your computer?

   _____

   Leave the Registry Editor open for the next exercise.

Exercise 2
Using the Find Key Command

In this exercise, you will use Registry Editor's Find Key command to search the registry to find a specific word in the key names in the registry.

▶   **To use the Find Key command**

1. In the HKEY_LOCAL_MACHINE On Local Machine window, click the HKEY_LOCAL_MACHINE subkey to ensure that the entire subtree is searched.

2. On the View menu, click Find Key.

   The Find dialog box appears.

3. In the Find What text box, type **windows**.

4. Click the Find Next button, and wait for the first matching entry to appear. This may take a few seconds.

5. Continue clicking the Find Next button until a Warning dialog box appears, indicating that the Registry Editor can't find the desired key.

   Notice that this key appears in multiple locations in the registry.

6. Click OK to close the Warning dialog box.

7. Click Cancel to close the Find dialog box.

8. Close the Registry Editor.

9. Log off the computer.

Exercise 3
Viewing the Registry Settings of a Remote Computer

In this exercise, you will work in pairs to view the registry settings on a remote computer.

▶ **To view the registry settings on a remote computer**

1. Log on to the domain as Student*z* using a password of "password".

2. Click the Start button, and then click Run.

3. In the Open combo box, type **regedt32** and then click OK.

4. The Registry Editor starts.

5. Maximize the Registry Editor window.

6. On the Registry menu, click Select Computer.

   The Select Computer dialog box appears.

7. Under Select Computer, select Computer*p* (the name of your partner's computer) in the list of computers under Corp*y* and then click OK.

   A Warning dialog box appears, indicating that AutoRefresh is not available for remote computers.

8. Click OK to close the Warning dialog box.

   How many subtrees are displayed for the remote computer?

   _____

   _____

9. On the Window menu, click HKEY_USERS On Computer*p*.

   The HKEY_ USERS On Computer*p* window appears in the Registry Editor. The HKEY_USERS subtree contains all actively loaded user profiles. Notice there are three entries under HKEY_USERS:

   - The DEFAULT entry stores the profile used when no user is logged on to the computer (for example, when the Welcome To Windows dialog box is displayed).

   - The next entry starts with an S and contains a series of numbers and dashes. This is the Security Identifier (SID) of the user currently logged on to the local computer. In this case, it is the SID for your partner.

   - The third entry contains your partner's SID with a Classes extension. Microsoft Windows 2000 allows the system to register program classes independently for each user. This is known as per-user class registration.

10. On the Window menu, click HKEY_LOCAL_MACHINE On Computer*p*.

    The HKEY_LOCAL_MACHINE On Computer*p* window appears in the Registry Editor.

11. Expand the SOFTWARE\Microsoft\Windows NT\CurrentVersion subkey.

    What is the current build number of the Windows 2000 Professional software installed on your partner's computer?

    _____

12. Under the SOFTWARE\Microsoft\Windows NT\CurrentVersion subkey, double-click NetworkCards.

    How many network adapter cards are in your partner's computer and what types of cards are installed?

    _____

    _____

13. Close the Registry Editor.

Lab 6: Working with Dynamic Storage

Objectives

After completing this lab, you will be able to

- Upgrade a basic disk to a dynamic disk.
- Create a simple volume.
- Create a custom MMC console containing Disk Management for remote administration.
- Use Disk Management to extend a volume on a remote computer.

Estimated time to complete this lab: 50 minutes

Exercise 1
Upgrading a Disk

In this exercise, you will use Disk Management to upgrade a basic disk to a dynamic disk.

▶   **To upgrade a basic disk**

1. Log on locally to Computer$z$ as Administrator with a password of "password".
2. Right-click My Computer, and then click Manage.

    The Computer Management window appears.
3. In the console tree, under Storage, click Disk Management.

    Notice that the storage type of Disk 0 is Basic.

Note If the Upgrade Disk wizard starts automatically, click Cancel. This might occur if your computer contains a disk configured for basic storage that does not contain the Microsoft Windows 2000 Professional boot partition.

---

4. In the lower-right pane of the Computer Management window, right-click Disk 0 and then click Properties.

    The Disk 0 Properties dialog box appears.

    What is the type of disk 0?

    _____

    What is the capacity of disk 0, and how much unallocated space is there on disk 0?

    _____

5. Under Volumes Contained On This Disk, click (C:) and then click the Properties button.

    The Local Disk (C:) Properties dialog box appears.

    What is the Capacity, Used Space, and Free Space on volume C:?

    _____

6. Click Cancel to close the Local Disk (C:) Properties dialog box.
7. Click Cancel to close the Disk 0 Properties dialog box.
8. In the lower-right pane of the Computer Management window, right-click Disk 0 and then click Upgrade To Dynamic Disk.

    The Upgrade To Dynamic Disk dialog box appears.
9. Make sure that Disk 0 is the only disk selected for upgrade, and then click OK.

    The Disks To Upgrade dialog box appears.

10. Click the Details button.

    The Upgrade Details dialog box appears. This dialog box presents a graphical display of the disks selected to be upgraded and all the volumes contained on each disk.

11. Click OK to close the Upgrade Details dialog box.

12. On the Disks To Upgrade dialog box, click the Upgrade button.

    A Disk Management dialog box appears, warning that after this upgrade you will not be able to boot previous versions of Windows from any volumes on this disk.

Caution If you are dual booting with another operating system (for example, Microsoft Windows 95 or Windows 98) loaded on drive C, these operating systems will no longer run. Only Windows 2000 can access a dynamic drive.

13. Click the Yes button.

    An Upgrade Disks dialog box appears, notifying you that file systems on any of the disks to be upgraded will be force-dismounted.

14. Click the Yes button.

    A Confirm message box appears, notifying you that a reboot will take place to complete the upgrade process.

15. Click OK.

    Your computer restarts.

▶ **To confirm the upgrade**

1. Log on locally to Computerz as Administrator with a password of "password".

Note If a System Settings Change message box appears, prompting you to restart your computer, click the Yes button. After the computer restarts and you log on as Administrator, if you see this same System Settings Change message box again prompting you to restart your computer, click the No button. Restarting the computer again is not necessary.

2. Click the Start button, point to Programs, point to Administrative Tools, and click Computer Management.

    The Computer Management window appears.

3. In the console tree, under Storage, click Disk Management.

Note If your computer has more than one disk, the Upgrade Disk wizard might appear. If it does, click Cancel to close it.

Notice that the storage type of Disk 0 is now Dynamic.

Leave the Disk Management window open for the next exercise.

Exercise 2
Creating a Simple Volume

In this exercise, you will use Disk Management to create a new simple volume.

▶   **To create a new simple volume**

1. In the Disk Management window, right-click the remaining unallocated space on Disk 0 in the lower-right pane and then click Create Volume.

   The Create Volume wizard appears.

2. Click Next.

   The Select Volume Type page appears.

   Notice that Simple Volume is the only available option.

3. Click Next.

   The Select Disks page appears. The value in the For Selected Disks text box represents the remaining free space on Drive 0.

4. Set the volume size to an appropriate size based on the amount of space available (25 MB is plenty to create the new volume, but be sure to leave at least 25 MB free for use later on), and then click Next.

   The Assign Drive Letter Or Path page appears.

5. Ensure that the Assign A Drive Letter radio button is selected, and in the drop-down list, select N to assign the drive letter N to the new volume.

6. Click Next.

   The Format Volume page appears.

7. Ensure that Format This Volume As Follows is selected and that File System To Use is set to NTFS.

8. Type **Volume** *z* (where z is your assigned student number) in the Volume Label text box.

9. Select the Perform A Quick Format radio button, and then click Next.

   The Completing The Create Volume Wizard page appears.

10. Read the information on the Completing The Create Volume Wizard page, and then click Finish.

    It will take a minute or two for Windows 2000 Professional to create and format the new volume. Notice that Volume*z* now appears on Disk 0.

11. Close all open windows, and then log off.

Exercise 3
Creating a Custom MMC Console Containing Disk Management for Remote Administration

In this exercise, you will use the Microsoft Management Console (MMC) to create a custom MMC console containing Disk Management and pointing to your partner's computer.

▶ **To create a remote administration customized console**

1. Log on to the domain as Student$z$ (where z is your student number) with a password of "password".

2. Click the Start button, click Run, type **mmc**, and then click OK.

   The Microsoft Management Console starts.

3. Maximize the Console1 window and the Console Root window.

4. On the Console menu, click Add/Remove Snap-In.

   The Add/Remove Snap-In dialog box appears.

5. Click the Add button.

   The Add Standalone Snap-In dialog box appears.

6. Select Disk Management, and then click the Add button.

   The Disk Management dialog box appears.

7. Click Another Computer, and then click the Browse button.

8. In the Select Computer dialog box, double-click Computer$p$ (your partner's computer).

9. Click the Finish button on the Disk Management dialog box.

10. Close the Add Standalone Snap-In dialog box.

11. Click OK to close the Add/Remove Snap-In dialog box.

12. On the Console menu, click Save As.

13. In the File Name text box, type **Remote Disk Man** and then click the Save button.

14. On the Console menu, click Exit.

Exercise 4
Using Disk Management on a Remote Computer

In this exercise, you will use Disk Management to extend a volume on your partner's computer.

Note You will work in pairs for this exercise. When the first partner has completed the exercise, swap roles and repeat the procedures.

▶ **To use Disk Management to extend a volume on a remote computer**

1. Click the Start button, click Run, type **mmc**, and click OK.

2. On the Console menu, click Open and then double-click Remote Disk Man.

3. Maximize the Console1 window and the Console Root window.

4. In the left pane on your computer, select Disk Management (Computer$p$) (where p is your partner's student number). Click Storage, and then click Disk Management in order to run Disk Management for your partner's computer on your machine.

5. Right-click Volume$p$, and then click Extend Volume.

   The Welcome To The Extend Volume Wizard page appears.

6. Click Next.

   The Select Disk page appears.

7. In the For Selected Disks text box, type **25** and then click Next.

   The Completing The Extend Volume Wizard page appears.

8. Click the Finish button.

   You have just extended a volume on a remote computer.

9. Click one of the two 25 MB volumes, and notice that the two volumes are both selected.

10. Close Remote Disk Man.

    A MMC dialog box asks if you would like to save the console settings for Remote Disk Man.

11. Click the Yes button, and then log off.

12. Your partner should run Computer Management on his/her computer and verify that the volume was extended.

    On the right-hand side under the volume, you can scroll and see that the size of Volume 1 (N:) has increased. At the bottom of the right-hand side, you should see what appears to be two volumes labeled Volume$z$ (N:) but in reality is the extended volume. If you cannot read the label, point to it with your mouse pointer. To verify that the two volumes are actually functioning as one volume, click either volume labeled Volume$z$ (N:) and notice that both volumes are selected.

Lab 7: Configuring TCP/IP

Objectives

After completing this lab, you will be able to

- Verify a computer's TCP/IP configuration.
- Configure TCP/IP to use a static IP address and a static DNS server address.
- Configure TCP/IP to obtain an IP address by using DHCP and to obtain a DNS server address automatically.
- Verify that an IP address was assigned by Automatic Private IP Addressing and test connectivity.

Estimated time to complete this lab: 50 minutes

Note TCP/IP should be the only installed protocol on your computer.

Exercise 1
Verifying a Computer's TCP/IP Configuration

In this exercise, you will use two TCP/IP utilities, ipconfig and ping, to verify your computer's TCP/IP configuration.

Note As you complete the exercises in this lab, you will use the Command Prompt and Network Connections windows frequently. For the sake of efficiency, you will open the windows one time and then minimize and maximize them as necessary.

▶ **To verify a computer's TCP/IP configuration**

1. Log on locally to Computerz as Administrator with a password of "password".

2. Click the Start button, point to Programs, point to Accessories, and then click Command Prompt.

3. At the command prompt, type **ipconfig /all** and then press ENTER.

   The Windows 2000 IP Configuration utility displays the TCP/IP configuration of the physical and logical adapters configured on your computer.

4. The ipconfig command displays two sections of information: Windows 2000 IP Configuration and Ethernet Adapter Local Area Connection. Use the information displayed in both of these sections to complete the following table.

Setting	Value
Host name	
Description	_Realtek RTL 8029 Ethernet_
Physical address	_00-20-18-2B-3F-42_
DHCP enabled	_Yes_
Autoconfiguration enabled	
IP address	_192.168.0.2_
Subnet mask	_255.255.255.0_
Default gateway	_192.168.0.1_
DNS Server	

5. To verify that the IP address is correctly installed and bound to your adapter, at the command prompt, type **ping 127.0.0.1** and then press ENTER.

A response similar to the following indicates a successful ping:

```
Pinging 127.0.0.1 with 32 bytes of data:
Reply from 127.0.0.1: bytes=32 time<10ms TTL=128
Reply from 127.0.0.1: bytes=32 time<10ms TTL=128
Reply from 127.0.0.1: bytes=32 time<10ms TTL=128
Reply from 127.0.0.1: bytes=32 time<10ms TTL=128
Ping statistics for 127.0.0.1:
    Packets: Sent = 4,  Received = 4,  Lost  = 0 <0% loss>,
Approximate round trip times in milliseconds:
    Minimum = 0ms,  Maximum = 0ms,  Average = 0ms
```

6. Minimize the Command Prompt window.

Exercise 2
Configuring TCP/IP to Use a Static IP Address and to Use a Static DNS Server Address

In this exercise, you will determine if installing Microsoft Windows 2000 Professional using the typical settings for configuring network components configures TCP/IP to use a static IP address or to obtain an IP address by using DHCP. You will then manually configure TCP/IP to use a static IP address and a static DNS server address. Finally you will ping your partner's IP address to confirm that you have correctly configured TCP/IP.

Note In this exercise, you will be working in pairs.

▶ **To configure TCP/IP to use a static IP address and a static DNS server address**

1. Right-click My Network Places, and then click Properties.

   The Network And Dial-Up Connections window appears.

2. Right-click Local Area Connection, and then click Properties.

   The Local Area Connection Properties dialog box appears, displaying the network adapter in use and the network components used in this connection.

3. Click Internet Protocol (TCP/IP), and then verify that the check box to the left of the entry is selected.

4. Click the Properties button.

   The Internet Protocol (TCP/IP) Properties dialog box appears.

   How does installing Windows 2000 Professional using the typical settings for configuring network components configure TCP/IP? In other words, is TCP/IP configured to obtain an IP address by using DHCP or by using a static IP address?

   _____

   _____

5. Select the Use The Following IP Address radio button.

6. To determine the IP address you should use for your static IP address, add 100 to your student number and use that as the last field in the following IP address: 10.1.1.*a*.

   For example, if your student number is 21, you would use the following IP address: 10.1.1.121

7. In the IP Address text box, type the IP address you calculated in step 6.

8. In the Subnet Mask text box, type **255.255.0.0**.

9. Leave the Default Gateway text box empty unless your instructor provides a default gateway to use during class.

Important Be careful when manually entering IP configuration settings, especially numeric addresses. The most frequent cause of TCP/IP connection problems is incorrect IP address information.

10. Select the Use The Following DNS Server Address radio button.

Important There are two choices to configure your DNS client. Selecting Obtain DNS Server Address Automatically will supply the network addresses for the DNS servers on the network if there are any servers available. However, you will select Use The Following DNS Server Addresses for the purposes of this lab. This allows you to specify the DNS server address your client will be using.

11. In the Preferred DNS Server text box, type the IP address of the primary name server for this client.

Important Ask your instructor for the IP address of the primary DNS server. It is probably the IP address of the Instructor computer, 10.1.1.100, but the address can vary depending on the classroom setup.

12. If a second DNS server is available for this client, in the Alternate DNS Server text box, type the IP address of the second name server for this client.

Important Ask your instructor if there is a secondary DNS server, and if so, what its address is.

Tip A client will attempt to first send its query request to the preferred name server. If that name server isn't responding, the client will send the query request to the alternate name server. If you're going to configure several computers running Windows 2000 Professional as DNS clients, configure some of the clients to use the alternate name server as the preferred name server. This reduces the load on the primary server.

13. Click OK to close the Internet Protocol (TCP/IP) Properties dialog box.

    You are returned to the Local Area Connection Properties dialog box.

14. Click OK to close the Local Area Connection Properties dialog box.

15. Minimize the Network And Dial-Up Connections window.

▶   **To test the static TCP/IP configuration**

1. Maximize the Command Prompt window.

2. To verify that the IP address is working and configured for your adapter, type **ping** *your_partner's_IP_address* at the command prompt and then press ENTER.

   What happens?

   _____

   _____

   _____

   _____

   _____

   _____

   _____

   _____

   _____

   _____

3. If you were able to successfully ping your partner's IP address, minimize the Command Prompt window. If you weren't able to successfully ping your partner's IP address, verify that your IP address and subnet mask are correct.

Exercise 3
Configuring TCP/IP to Automatically Obtain an IP Address and a DNS Server Address

In this exercise, you will configure TCP/IP to automatically obtain an IP address and to automatically obtain a DNS server address.

▶ **To configure TCP/IP to automatically obtain an IP address and a DNS server address**

1. Maximize the Network And Dial-Up Connections window, right-click Local Area Connection, and then click Properties.

   The Local Area Connection Properties dialog box appears.

2. Click Internet Protocol (TCP/IP), and then verify that the check box to the left of the entry is selected.

3. Click the Properties button.

   The Internet Protocol (TCP/IP) Properties dialog box appears.

4. Select the Obtain An IP Address Automatically radio button.

5. Select the Obtain DNS Server Address Automatically radio button.

6. Click OK to close the Internet Protocol (TCP/IP) Properties dialog box.

7. Click OK to close the Local Area Connection Properties dialog box.

8. Minimize the Network And Dial-Up Connections window.

   How can you determine the IP address assigned to your computer? What is the IP address assigned to your computer?

   _____

   _____

   _____

   _____

Exercise 4
Obtaining an IP Address by Using Automatic Private IP Addressing

For this exercise, your instructor will have disabled the DHCP server. Without a DHCP server available to provide an IP address, the Windows 2000 Automatic Private IP Addressing feature will provide a unique IP address for your computer.

Note In this exercise, you will be working in pairs.

▶ **To obtain an IP address by using Automatic Private IP Addressing**

1. At the command prompt, type **ipconfig /release** and then press ENTER.

2. At the command prompt, type **ipconfig /renew** and then press ENTER.

   There will be a pause while Windows 2000 attempts to locate a DHCP server on the network.

   What message appears, and what does it indicate?

   _____

   _____

   _____

   How can you determine what IP address is assigned to your computer? What is the IP address assigned to your computer?

   _____

   _____

   _____

   _____

   Is this the same IP address assigned to your computer in Exercise 3? Why or why not?

   _____

   _____

3. Test TCP/IP connectivity with your partner's computer. Type **ping** *your_partner's_IP_address* at the command prompt, and then press ENTER.

   Were you successful? Why or why not?

   _____

   _____

Exercise 5
Obtaining an IP Address by Using DHCP

In this exercise, you will obtain an IP address from a DHCP server.

Important Before you begin this exercise, confirm that your instructor has enabled the DHCP service.

▶ **To obtain an IP address by using DHCP**

1. At the command prompt, type **ipconfig /renew** and then press ENTER.

   After a short wait, the Ethernet Adapter Local Area Connection information is displayed.

2. Verify that the DHCP server has assigned an IP address to your computer.

3. Close the Command Prompt window.

Lab 8: Installing Additional Protocols

Objectives

After completing this lab, you will be able to

- Install the NetBEUI Protocol.

Estimated time to complete this lab: 10 minutes

Exercise 1
Installing NetBEUI

In this exercise, you will install the NetBEUI Protocol.

Note You can install any of the available protocols in Windows 2000 by using this procedure.

▶ **To install the NetBEUI Protocol**

1. Maximize the Network And Dial-Up Connections window.

2. Right-click Local Area Connection, and then click Properties.

   The Local Area Connection Properties dialog box appears, displaying the network adapter in use and the network components used in this connection.

3. Click the Install button.

   The Select Network Component Type dialog box appears.

4. Click Protocol, and then click the Add button.

   The Select Network Protocol dialog box appears.

   What protocols can you install?

   _____

   _____

   _____

   _____

   _____

5. Select NetBEUI Protocol, and then click OK.

   Notice that NetBEUI Protocol is added to the Components list in the Local Area Connection Properties dialog box that appears.

6. If you are prompted to reboot the computer, reboot the computer. If you are not prompted to reboot the computer, then close all open dialog boxes and windows and log off.

Lab 9: Working with Network Bindings

Objectives

After completing this lab, you will be able to

- Change the binding order of a protocol.
- Unbind a protocol from a network adapter card.
- Uninstall a protocol.
- Bind a protocol to a network adapter card.

Estimated time to complete this lab: 15 minutes

Exercise 1
Changing the Binding Order of a Protocol

In this exercise, you will change the binding order of the protocols bound to your network adapter card.

▶ **To change the protocol binding order**

1. Log on locally to Computerz as Administrator with a password of "password".
2. Right-click My Network Places, and then click Properties.
3. In the Network And Dial-Up Connections window, click the Advanced button and then click Advanced Settings.

   The Advanced Settings dialog box appears.

   What is the order of the protocols listed under Client For Microsoft Networks in the Bindings For Local Area Connection list?

   _____

   _____

4. Under Client For Microsoft Networks, select NetBEUI Protocol.
5. Click the Down button.

   Notice that the order of the protocols listed under Client For Microsoft Networks has changed. The NetBEUI Protocol should now be listed below Internet Protocol (TCP/IP). If it's not, click the Down button again to move it below Internet Protocol (TCP/IP).

   Leave the Advanced Settings dialog box open for the next exercise.

Exercise 2
Unbinding a Protocol

In this exercise, you will unbind TCP/IP from your network adapter card, which will leave NetBEUI as the only protocol available to access other computers.

▶ **To unbind TCP/IP**

1. In the Advanced Settings dialog box, under Client For Microsoft Networks in the Bindings For Local Area Connection list, unbind Internet Protocol (TCP/IP) by clearing the check box to the left of the entry.

   TCP/IP is now unbound from your network adapter card.

2. Click OK to close the Advanced Settings dialog box.

Exercise 3
Uninstalling NetBEUI

In this exercise, you will uninstall NetBEUI.

▶   **To remove NetBEUI**

1. In the Network And Dial-Up Connections window, right-click Local Area Connection and then click Properties.

   The Local Area Connection Properties dialog box appears, displaying the adapter in use and the network components configured for this connection.

2. Click NetBEUI Protocol, and then click the Uninstall button.

   The Uninstall NetBEUI Protocol dialog box appears.

3. Click the Yes button to continue.

   The Local Network dialog box appears, indicating that your computer must be rebooted before the new settings take effect.

4. Click the No button. You do not want to reboot at this time.

   Notice that NetBEUI Protocol is no longer listed as an installed protocol.

5. Close the Local Area Connections Properties dialog box.

   The Local Network dialog box appears, again indicating that your computer must be restarted before the new settings take effect.

6. Click the No button. You do not want to restart your computer at this time.

   TCP/IP is now the only protocol installed on your computer.

Exercise 4
Binding a Protocol

In this exercise, you will bind TCP/IP to your network adapter card.

▶ **To bind TCP/IP**

1. On the Advanced menu of the Network And Dial-Up Connections window, click Advanced Settings.

   The Advanced Settings dialog box appears.

2. Under Client For Microsoft Networks, select Internet Protocol (TCP/IP) by selecting the check box to the left of the option.

3. Click OK.

4. Close the Network And Dial-Up Connections window.

   TCP/IP is now bound to your network adapter card.

5. Restart your computer to put into effect the changes you made in exercises 3 and 4.

Lab 10: Searching Microsoft Windows 2000 Active Directory Directory Services

Objectives

After completing this lab, you will be able to

- Search Active Directory directory services.

Estimated time to complete this lab: 15 minutes

Exercise 1
Searching Active Directory Directory Services for a Computer

In this exercise, you will learn how to search Active Directory directory services for a computer.

▶ **To search Active Directory directory services for a computer**

1. Log on to the Corp*y* domain as Student*z* with a password of "password".

Note Replace the *y* in Corp*y* with the number your instructor told you to use. Replace the *z* in Student*z* with your student number.

---

2. Right-click My Network Places, and then click Properties.

   The Network And Dial-Up Connections window appears.

3. Click the Search button at the top of the window.

   The Search pane appears on the left side of the Network And Dial-Up Connections window.

4. Scroll down until you see Search For Other Items.

5. Select Computers under Search For Other Items.

   The Computer Name text box appears.

6. In the Computer Name text box type **Instructor*x***, where *x* is the number of the instructor's computer.

7. Click the Search Now button.

   The Search Results – Computers pane appears on the right side of the Search Results – Computers window showing the instructor's computer located in the Corp*y* domain.

8. Double-click Instructor*x*.

   In the right pane, you see the shared resources available on the instructor's computer, replacing the Search Results – Computers pane. These resources should include the following three shared folders: W2000Pro, Public, and Users. You should also see a shared printer: HPLaserJ.

   You have just searched Active Directory directory services for and located a computer.

9. In the Computer Name text box in the left-hand pane, type **Computer*p***, where *p* is your partner's student number.

10. Click the Search Now button.

    The Search Results – Computers pane appears on the right side of the window showing the name of your partner's computer with the location of the computer being in the Corp*y* domain.

11. In the Search Results – Computers pane, double-click Computer*p* (your partner's computer).

    Shared resources on your partner's computer are displayed in the right-hand pane, replacing the Search Results – Computers pane.

    Leave the Search window open.

Exercise 2
Searching Active Directory Directory Services for a User

In this exercise, you will learn how to search Active Directory directory services for a user.

▶   **To search Active Directory directory services for a user**

1. In the left-hand pane, under Search For Other Items, click People.

    The Find People dialog box appears.

2. Click the Question Mark (?) button in the upper right-hand corner of the dialog box.

    Notice that a question mark is attached to your mouse pointer.

3. Point to the Name text box, and click.

    What can you type in this text box to search for other than a contact name?

    _____

    _____

Tip Whenever you see a question mark in the upper right-hand corner of a dialog box or window, you can use it to get information about the screen.

4. Click anywhere on the screen to clear the reply to your request for information.

5. In the Name text box, type **Student*p***, where *p* is your partner's student number.

6. In the Look In drop-down list, select Active Directory.

7. Click the Find Now button.

    Search displays Student*p* in the list box that appears at the bottom of the Find People window. You can click the Properties button to look at additional information about Student*p* in the Properties dialog box, or you can click the Add To Address Book button to add the name to your Address Book.

8. Close the Find People dialog box.

    Close all open windows, and then log off the domain.

Lab 11: Creating Local User Accounts

Objectives

After completing this lab, you will be able to

- Create local user accounts.

Estimated time to complete this lab: 15 minutes

Exercise 1
Creating Local User Accounts

In this exercise, you will create the four local user accounts shown in the following table:

User name	Full name	Password	Change password
User1	User One	(blank)	Must
User2	User Two	(blank)	(blank)
User3	User Three	User3	Must
User4	User Four	User4	(blank)

Important Your computer is running Microsoft Windows 2000 Professional and is part of a domain. Ordinarily, you would not create local user accounts in a domain, as the domain does not recognize local user accounts and a user would be unable to access resources in the domain. However, for the purposes of this class, you will create local user accounts in order to become familiar with the process.

The following procedure outlines the steps required to use the Computer Management snap-in to create the first user account. After you have created the first user account, follow the same steps to create the remaining user accounts. Use the information in the table to set them up.

▶ **To create local user accounts**

1. Log on locally to Computerz (where z is your student number) as Administrator using a password of "password".

2. Click the Start button, point to Programs, point to Administrative Tools, and then click Computer Management.

   The Computer Management Snap-In window appears.

3. Expand Local Users And Groups.

4. Under Local Users And Groups, right-click Users, and then click New User.

   The New User dialog box appears.

5. In the User Name text box, type **User1**.

6. In the Full Name text box, type **User One**.

7. In the Password text box and the Confirm Password text box, type the password shown in the table, or leave these boxes blank if you aren't assigning a password.

Note Any assigned password is displayed as asterisks as you type. This prevents onlookers from viewing the password as it is entered.

8. Specify whether or not the user can change his or her password.

Note In high-security environments, assign initial passwords to user accounts and then require users to change their password the next time they log on. This prevents a user account from existing without a password, and once the user logs on and changes his or her password, only the user will know the password.

---

9. After you have selected the appropriate password options, click the Create button.

10. Complete steps 5 through 9 for the remaining user accounts.

11. When you finish creating user accounts, close the New User dialog box.

12. Close the Computer Management window.

Exercise 2
Testing a New Local User Account

In this exercise, you test the User1 local user account you created in Exercise 1.

Important Only test and log on as User1. You will test and use the other local user accounts later in this Lab Manual.

▶ **To test a local user account**

1. Log off as Administrator.

2. Log on to the domain Corpy as User1 with no password.

   Were you successful? Why or why not?

   _____

   _____

   _____

   _____

3. Log on to your local computer, Computer*z* (where *z* is your student ID number), as User1 with no password.

4. When prompted to change User1's password, click OK to close the Logon Message dialog box.

5. Leave the Old Password text box empty. In the Password and Confirm Password text boxes, type **password** and then click OK.

   The Change Password dialog box appears to inform you that the password is changed.

6. Click OK.

   The Getting Started With Windows 2000 dialog box appears.

7. Click the Exit button to close the Getting Started With Windows 2000 dialog box.

8. Click the Start button, point to Programs, point to Administrative Tools, and then click Computer Management.

   Were you able to start Computer Management? Why or why not?

   _____

   _____

9. Create a custom Microsoft Management Console (MMC) console containing Computer Management, and then create a User5 with a password of User5.

Note If you have forgotten how to create a custom MMC console, see Lab 2: Creating a Customized Console with Microsoft Management Console.

Were you able to create a custom MMC console containing Computer Management?

_____

_____

Were you able to create User5? Why or why not?

_____

_____

_____

10. Log off the computer.

Lab 12: Creating and Managing Local Groups

Objectives

After completing this lab, you will be able to

- Create local groups.
- Add user accounts to and remove user accounts from local groups.
- Use the CTRL key and the SHIFT key to select groups of users to be added to or deleted from local groups.

Estimated time to complete this lab: 15 minutes

Exercise 1
Creating Local Groups

In this exercise, you will create two local groups, Engineering and HelpDesk.

Important Your computers are running Microsoft Windows 2000 Professional and are part of a domain. Ordinarily, you would not create local groups in a domain, as the domain does not recognize local groups and a user would be unable to access resources in the domain. However, for the purposes of this class, you will create local groups to become familiar with the process.

▶ **To create a local user group**

1. Log on locally to Computer$z$ (where z is your student number) as Administrator using a password of "password".

2. Click the Start button, point to Programs, point to Administrative Tools, and then click Computer Management.

   The Computer Management Snap-In window appears.

3. Expand Local Users And Groups, and then click Groups.

   In the Details pane, Computer Management displays a list of current and built-in local groups.

   What groups currently exist? Double-click each group and record the members of that group.

   _____

   _____

   _____

   _____

   _____

   _____

   _____

   _____

4. If any of the group Properties dialog boxes are open, close them. Right-click Groups, and then click New Group.

   The New Group dialog box appears.

5. Click the Question Mark (?) button in the upper right-hand corner of the dialog box, and then click the Group Name text box.

   According to the message that appears, how many characters can a group name contain? What character is illegal?

   _____

   _____

6. In the Group Name text box, type **Engineers**, and then in the Description text box, type **Engineering Design Team**.

7. Click the Question Mark (?) button in the upper right-hand corner of the dialog box, and then click the Members list box.

   According to the message that appears, which user accounts can be members of this group?

   _____

   _____

   _____

   _____

   _____

   _____

8. Click the Add button.

   The Select Users Or Groups dialog box appears.

9. Scroll down the name list until you see User1 and User4. Click User1 to select it.

10. Click User4.

    What happens when you click User4?

    _____

11. Click User1 to select it. Hold the CTRL key down, and click User4.

    What happens when you hold down the CTRL key and click User4?

    _____

12. Click the Add button.

    Computerz\User1 and Computerz\User4 should be shown in the list box below the Add button.

Note Replace the z in Computerz with your student number.

13. Click OK.

    In the New Group dialog box, notice that User1 and User4 are shown in the Members list box.

14. Click the Create button.

15. Close the New Group dialog box.

    Notice that Windows 2000 created the group and added it to the list of groups.

16. Create a group named HelpDesk. Type **Access to Resolved Database** in the Description text box. Instead of holding down the CTRL key after you select User1 and while you click User4, hold down the SHIFT key.

What happens when you hold down the SHIFT key and click User4?

_____

What users are members of the HelpDesk group?

_____

Notice that the Engineers and HelpDesk groups are listed in the Details pane.

Exercise 2
Adding Members to and Removing Members
from an Existing Group

In this exercise, you will add the User2 and User3 local user accounts that you created in Exercise 1 of Lab 11 to the local group Engineers.

▶ **To add user accounts to a local group**

1. In the Details pane of the Computer Management snap-in, double-click Engineers.

   The Engineers Properties dialog box displays the properties of the group. Notice that User1 and User4 are shown in the Members list box.

2. To add a member to the group, click the Add button.

   The Select Users Or Groups dialog box appears.

3. In the Name list box, scroll down until you find User2 and User3.

   Should you hold down the CTRL key after you select User2 and while you click User3, or should you hold down the SHIFT key? Why?

   _____

   _____

   _____

   _____

   _____

4. Add User2 and User3 to the Engineers group.

   The Engineers Properties dialog box shows User1, User2, User3, and User4 in the Members list box.

5. Click the Apply button, and then close the Engineers Properties dialog box.

   You have just added User2 and User3 to the Engineers group.

▶ **To remove user accounts from a local group**

1. In the Details pane of the Computer Management snap-in, double-click Engineers.

   The Engineers Properties dialog box displays the properties of the group. Notice that User1, User2, User3, and User4 are shown in the Members list box.

2. Select User1 and User4, and then click the Remove button.

   Notice that User1 and User4 are no longer shown in the Members list box.

   Should you use the CTRL key or the SHIFT key to select only User1 and User4 for deletion?

   _____

3. Click the Apply button, and then close the Engineers Properties dialog box.

   You have just removed the User1 and the User4 user accounts from the Engineers group. User1 and User4 still exist as local user accounts, but they are no longer members of the Engineers group.

4. Close Computer Management, and log off.

Lab 13: Installing a Network Printer

Objectives

After completing this lab, you will be able to

- Add and share a local printer.

Estimated time to complete this lab: 15 minutes

Important You do not have to have a print device to complete this lab.

Exercise 1
Installing a Network Printer

In this exercise, you will use the Add Printer wizard to install a local printer and share the printer.

▶ **To add a local printer**

1. Log on locally to Computer*z* (where *z* is your student number) as Administrator using a password of "password".

2. Click the Start button, point to Settings, and then click Printers.

   The Printers window appears. If your computer has a fax modem installed, a Fax icon appears in the Printer system folder.

3. Double-click the Add Printer icon.

4. In the Add Printer wizard, click Next.

   The Add Printer wizard prompts you for the location of the printer.

Note Because you are creating the printer on the computer at which you are sitting and not on a different computer, this printer is referred to as a *local printer*.

---

5. Ensure the Local Printer radio button is selected, clear the Automatically Detect And Install My Plug And Play Printer check box, and then click Next.

Note Which port types are available depends on the installed network protocols. For this exercise, assume that the print device that you are adding is directly attached to your computer and using the LPT1 port.

---

6. Ensure that the Use The Following Port radio button is selected, and then under Use The Following Port, ensure that LPT1 is selected.

Note If the print device is connected to a port that is not listed, select the Create A New Port radio button and then enter the port type.

---

7. Click Next.

   The wizard prompts you for the printer manufacturer and model. You will add an HP LaserJet 5Si printer.

Tip The list of printers is sorted in alphabetical order. If you can't find a printer name, make sure that you are looking in the correct location.

---

8. In the Manufacturers list box, select HP; in the Printers list box, select HP LaserJet 5Si; and then click Next.

The Name Your Printer page appears. Notice that Windows 2000 automatically supplies a default printer name in the Printer Name text box and that the default name is HP LaserJet 5Si. Notice also that the printer you are creating is by default set to be the printer that all Microsoft Windows-based programs will be using as the default printer.

9. To accept the default printer name and to use this printer as the default printer for all Windows-based programs, click Next.

The Printer Sharing page appears, prompting you for printer-sharing information.

▶ **To share a local printer**

1. On the Printer Sharing page, select the Share As radio button.

Notice that you can assign a shared-printer name, even though you already supplied a printer name. The *shared-printer name* is used to identify a printer on the network. The *printer name* is a description that will appear with the printer's icon in the Printers system folder and in Active Directory directory services.

2. In the Share As text box, type **3EastMail** and then click Next.

The Location And Comment page appears.

Note If your computer running Windows 2000 Professional is part of a domain, Windows 2000 displays the values that you enter for Location and Comment when a user searches Active Directory directory services for a printer. Entering this information is optional, but it can help users locate the printers more easily.

---

3. In the Location text box, type **Third Floor East Mail Room** and then click Next.

The Print Test Page page appears, asking you whether you want to print a test page or not.

4. Select the No radio button, and then click Next.

The Completing The Add Printer Wizard page appears and provides a summary of your installation choices.

Note As you review the summary, you might notice an error in the information you specified for the printer. To modify these settings, click the Back button.

---

5. Confirm the summary of your installation choices, and then click the Finish button.

   Windows 2000 Professional will copy files from the *systemroot* folder.

Note If Windows 2000 Professional displays the File Needed dialog box, prompting you for the location of the Windows 2000 Professional distribution files, click Start and then click Run. In the Open combo box, type **\\Instructor*x*\W2000Pro** (where *x* is the number of the instructor's computer) and then click OK. Because you are not connected to the Corp*y* domain, the Enter Network Password dialog box appears. In the Connect As text box, type **Student*z*** (where *z* is your student number), and in the Password text box, type **password**. Click OK. Double-click \I386.

Windows 2000 Professional copies the printer files and creates the shared printer. An icon for the HP LaserJet 5Si printer appears in the Printers window.

Notice that Windows 2000 displays an open hand under the printer icon. This indicates that the printer is shared. Notice also the check mark just above the printer, which indicates that the printer is the default printer.

6. Close all open windows, and log off.

Lab 14: Managing Printers

Objectives

After completing this lab, you will be able to

- Assign a form to a paper tray.
- Set up a separator page.
- Take ownership of a printer.

Estimated time to complete this lab: 15 minutes

Important You do not have to have a print device to complete this lab.

Exercise 1
Assigning Forms to Paper Trays

In this exercise, you will assign a paper type (form) to a paper tray so that when users print to a specified form, the print job is automatically routed to and adjusted for the correct tray.

▶ **To assign forms to paper trays**

1. Log on locally to Computer$z$ (where z is your student number) as Administrator using a password of "password".

2. Click the Start button, point to Settings, and then click Printers.

3. Right-click the HP LaserJet 5Si icon, or the icon for the printer that you set up previously, and then click Properties.

4. In the HP LaserJet 5Si Properties dialog box, click the Device Settings tab.

   Notice that there are multiple selections under Form To Tray Assignment. Some of the selections are labeled Not Available because they depend on options that aren't installed.

5. Select Lower Paper Tray, and then select Legal from the Lower Paper Tray drop-down list.

Note Whenever a user prints on legal-size paper, Microsoft Windows 2000 will instruct the printer to use the lower paper tray.

6. Click the Apply button.

   Leave the HP LaserJet 5Si Properties dialog box open for the next exercise.

Exercise 2
Setting Up Separator Pages

In this exercise, you will set up a separator page to print between documents. This separator page includes the user's name and the date and time that the document was printed.

▶ **To set up a separator page**

1. Click the Advanced tab of the HP LaserJet 5Si Properties dialog box.

2. Click the Separator Page button.

   The Separator Page dialog box appears.

3. In the Separator Page dialog box, click the Browse button.

   Another Separator Page dialog box appears.

   What folder contains the separator pages?

   _____

4. Select Sysprint.sep, and then click the Open button.

   The selected separator page file's path appears in the first Separator Page dialog box.

5. Click OK.

   Windows 2000 will now print a separator page between print jobs.

6. Click OK to close the HP LaserJet 5Si Properties dialog box. Close the Printers window.

7. Log off the computer.

Exercise 3
Taking Ownership of a Printer

In this exercise, you will practice taking ownership of a printer.

▶ **To take ownership of a printer**

1. Log on to Corp*y* as Student*z* using a password of "password".

Important Replace the *y* in Corp*y* with the number your instructor tells you to use, and replace the *z* in Student*z* with your student number.

---

2. Click the Start button, point to Settings, and then click Printers.
3. Right-click the HP LaserJet 5Si icon, and then click Properties.
4. Click the Security tab of the HP LaserJet 5Si Properties dialog box.
5. On the Security tab, click the Advanced button, and then click the Owner tab.

    Who currently owns this printer?

    _____

6. To take ownership of the printer, in the Name list box, select the name you used to log on.

Note The name you used to log on should look something like the following: Student One (Student1@corp1.corp.com).

---

7. Click the Apply button.

    Who owns this printer now?

    _____

    _____

8. Click OK to close the Access Control Settings For HP LaserJet 5Si dialog box.
9. Click OK to close the HP LaserJet 5Si Properties dialog box, close the Printers window, and then log off your computer.

Lab 15: Managing Documents

Objectives

After completing this lab, you will be able to

- Take a printer offline.
- Set a notification.
- Increase the priority of a document.
- Cancel the printing of a document.

Estimated time to complete this lab: 15 minutes

Important You do not have to have a print device to complete this lab.

Exercise 1
Taking a Printer Offline and Printing a Test Document

Windows 2000 displays error messages when it attempts to send documents to a print device that is not connected to the computer. Taking a printer offline causes documents that you send to the printer to be held on the computer while the print device is not available.

In this exercise, you will take the printer you created in Exercise 1 of Lab 13 offline and then print a document. Taking the printer offline will eliminate error messages about unavailable print devices in later exercises.

▶ **To take a printer offline**

1. Log on locally to Computer$z$ (where z is your student number) as Administrator using a password of "password".

2. Click the Start button, point to Settings, and then click Printers.

3. In the Printers window, click the HP LaserJet 5Si icon.

Note If you installed a different printer in Lab 13, then click the name of the printer you installed.

4. On the File menu, select Use Printer Offline.

Note If you pull down the File menu again, you will notice that a check mark will now be displayed in front of Use Printer Offline.

5. Notice that Windows 2000 grays-out the icon to show that the printer is not available, and that the Status of the printer states Use Printer Offline.

▶ **To print a test document**

1. In the Printers window, double-click the HP LaserJet 5Si icon.

   The HP LaserJet 5Si – Use Printer Offline window appears.

   Notice that the list of documents to be sent to the print device is empty.

2. Click the Start button, point to Programs, point to Accessories, and then click Notepad.

   The Untitled – Notepad windows appears.

3. On the File menu, click Open.

   An Open dialog box appears.

4. In the Look In drop-down list, select the WINNT folder.

Note If you did not install Windows 2000 Professional in the default folder WINNT, use the name of the folder in which you did install it.

5. Scroll through the list of folders and files, and click Setuplog.

   The File Name combo box should now contain Setuplog.

6. Click the Open button.

   Microsoft Notepad displays the contents of the Setuplog.txt file.

7. On the File menu, click Print.

   A Print dialog box appears, allowing you to select the printer and print options. Notice that the file will be printed on HP LaserJet 5Si.

Note If you installed a different printer in Lab 13, the printer name will vary.

   The Print dialog box displays the location information that you entered when you created the printer, and it shows that the status of the printer is offline. You can also use this dialog box to search Active Directory directory services for a printer.

8. Click the Print button.

   A Notepad message box briefly displays a message, stating that the document is printing.

9. Close Notepad.

   In the HP LaserJet 5Si window, you will see that the document is waiting to be sent to the print device. Windows 2000 Professional holds the document because you took the printer offline; normally, the document would be sent to the print device.

   Leave the HP LaserJet 5Si – Use Printer Offline window open for the next exercise.

Exercise 2
Setting a Notification

In this exercise, you will set a notification.

▶   **To set a notification**

1. In the HP LaserJet 5Si – Use Printer Offline window, select Setuplog – Notepad and then click Properties in the Document menu.

Note If you installed a different printer in Lab 13, the printer name will vary.

The Setuplog – Notepad Document Properties dialog box appears with the General tab active.

Which user is specified in the Notify text box? Why?

_____

_____

2. In the Notify text box, type **User1** and then click the Apply button.

Note You have just set the notification to User1, so when the Setuplog document is printed, User1 will be notified. Normally you would click OK here to close the Setuplog – Notepad Document Properties dialog box, but leave it open for the next exercise.

Exercise 3
Increasing the Priority of a Document

In this exercise, you will increase the priority of a document queued to print.

▶   **To increase the priority of a document**

1. In the Setuplog – Notepad Document Properties dialog box, on the General tab, notice the default priority.

   What is the current priority? Is it the lowest or the highest priority?

   _____

2. In the Priority box, move the slider to the right to increase the priority of the document to 36 and then click OK.

   Nothing changes visibly in the HP LaserJet 5Si – Use Printer Offline window.

3. On the Printer menu, click Use Printer Offline to remove the check mark and then immediately click Use Printer Offline again.

Note If Windows 2000 Professional displays a Printers Folder dialog box with an error message informing you that the printer port is unavailable, complete the following exercise, and then, in the dialog box, click Cancel.

4. Check the status of Setuplog to confirm that Windows 2000 Professional has started to print this document.

Exercise 4
Canceling the Printing of a Document

In this exercise, you will cancel the printing of the document Setuplog.

▶   **To cancel a document from printing**

1. Select Setuplog in the document list in the printer's window.

2. On the Document menu, click Cancel.

    Notice that the Status column changes to Deleting. In about a minute, the file
    will be deleted and Setuplog will be removed from the document list.

Tip You can also cancel a document by selecting the document and then pressing
the DELETE key.

---

3. Close all open windows.

Lab 16: Planning and Assigning NTFS Permissions

Objectives

After completing this lab, you will be able to

- Plan NTFS folder and file permissions.
- Assign NTFS permissions to folders.
- Apply NTFS folder and file permissions to users and groups.
- Test NTFS permissions you have applied.

Before You Begin

There are two different scenarios in this lab. The first scenario is based on three local groups: Managers, Accounting, and Executives. The second scenario is based on the Leads, Technicians, and Directors local groups and the local users outlined in the following table. Before beginning the exercises that follow, create the local users and groups listed in the following table:

Group	User Account
Leads	User17 (the password is User17) Password change at the next logon not required. Member of the Leads group.
Technicians	User18 (the password is User18) Password change at the next logon not required. Member of the Technicians group.
Directors	User19 (the password is User19) Password change at the next logon not required. Member of the Technicians group.
	User20 (the password is User20) Password change at the next logon not required. Member of the Directors group.
	User21 (the password is User21) Password change at the next logon not required.
	User22 (the password is User22) Password change at the next logon not required.

Create the following folders on your computer:

- C:\TechApps
- C:\TechApps\Troubleshoot
- C:\TechApps\FixesDB
- C:\TechTips\OpenDB
- C:\News
- C:\News\Policies

Estimated time to complete this lab: 60 minutes

Exercise 1
Planning NTFS Permissions

In this exercise, you will plan how to assign NTFS permissions to folders and files on a computer running Microsoft Windows 2000, based on the following scenario.

▶   **Scenario**

The computer running Windows 2000 Professional is part of a workgroup. The default NTFS folder and file permissions are Full Control for the Everyone group. The figure below shows the folder and file structure used for this lab. Review the following security criteria and record the changes that you need to make to the NTFS folder and file permissions to meet this security criteria.

The folder and file structure for this lab.

To plan NTFS permissions, you must determine the following:

- Which local groups and which built-in groups to use
- What permissions users will require to gain access to folders and files
- Whether or not to clear the Allow Inheritable Permissions From Parent To Propagate To This Object check box for the folder or file to which you are assigning permissions.

Keep the following general guidelines in mind:

- NTFS permissions that are assigned to a folder are inherited by all of the folders and files it contains. For example, to assign permissions for all of the folders and files in the TechApps folder, you need only assign NTFS permissions to the TechApps folder.
- To assign more restrictive permissions to a folder or file that is inheriting permissions, you must either *deny* the unwanted permissions or *block inheritance* by clearing the Allow Inheritable Permissions From Parent To Propagate To This Object check box.

The decisions you make are based on the following criteria:

- In addition to the default built-in groups, you have created the following groups:
  - Technician
  - Leads
  - Directors
- You have created the following user accounts:
  - User17
  - User18
  - User19
  - User20
  - User21
  - User22
- Administrators require the Full Control permission for all folders and files.
- All users will run programs in the TechApps\Troubleshoot folder, but they should not be able to modify the files in the TechApps\Troubleshoot folder.
- Members of the Technicians group should be able to read the database files stored in the TechTips\OpenDB application folder by running the associated database application, as well as create new entries for newly opened problems in the appropriate databases.
- Members of the Leads and Directors groups should be able to read documents in the TechTips\OpenDB application folders by running the associated spreadsheet and database applications, but they should not be able to modify the files in this folder.
- Members of the Technicians, Leads, and Directors groups should be able to read documents in the TechApps\FixesDB application folder by running the associated database application, but they should not be able to modify the files in this folder.
- User22 and User23 should be able to modify and delete files in the TechApps\FixesDB application folders by running the associated database application.
- All users should be able to read and create files in the News folder.
- All users should be prevented from modifying files in the News\Policies folder.

  When you apply custom permissions to a folder or file, which default permission entry should you remove?

Complete the following table to plan and record your permissions:

Path	User Account or Group	NTFS Permissions	Block Inheritance (Yes/No)
TechApps	_____	_____	_____
	_____	_____	_____
	_____	_____	_____
	_____	_____	_____
	_____	_____	_____
TechApps\FixesDB	_____	_____	_____
	_____	_____	_____
	_____	_____	_____
	_____	_____	_____
	_____	_____	_____
TechApps\Troubleshoot	_____	_____	_____
	_____	_____	_____
	_____	_____	_____
	_____	_____	_____
	_____	_____	_____
TechTips	_____	_____	_____
	_____	_____	_____
	_____	_____	_____
	_____	_____	_____
	_____	_____	_____
TechTips\OpenDB	_____	_____	_____
	_____	_____	_____
	_____	_____	_____
	_____	_____	_____
	_____	_____	_____
News	_____	_____	_____
	_____	_____	_____
	_____	_____	_____
	_____	_____	_____
News\Policies	_____	_____	_____
	_____	_____	_____
	_____	_____	_____
	_____	_____	_____

Exercise 2
Assigning NTFS Permissions for the News Folder

In this exercise, you will assign NTFS permissions from the above scenario and test to make sure the results are correct.

▶ **To remove permissions from the Everyone group**

1. Log on locally to Computer$z$ (where z is your student number) as Administrator using a password of "password".

2. Right-click My Computer, and then click Explore.

3. Expand Local Disk (C:), right-click the News folder, and then click Properties.

   The News Properties dialog box appears, with the General tab active.

4. Click the Security tab to display the permissions for the News folder.

   The News Properties dialog box appears, with the Security tab active.

   What are the existing folder permissions?

   _____

   Notice that the currently allowed permissions can't be modified.

5. Under Name, select the Everyone group and then click Remove.

   What do you see?

   _____

   _____

   _____

6. Click OK to close the message box.

7. Clear the Allow Inheritable Permissions From Parent To Propagate To This Object check box to block permissions from being inherited.

   A Security dialog box appears, prompting you to copy the previously inherited permissions to the folder or remove all inherited permissions for the folder except those that you explicitly specify.

8. Click the Remove button.

   What are the existing folder permissions?

   _____

▶ **To assign permissions to the Users group for the News folder**

1. In the News Properties dialog box, click the Add button.

Note Normally in a domain environment, you do not use local user accounts. For purposes of this class, we are using local user accounts.

2. If the Enter Network Password dialog box appears, click Cancel to close the dialog box.

   The Select Users, Computers, Or Groups dialog box appears.

3. In the Look In drop-down list at the top of the dialog box, select your computer, Computerz.

Note The Look In drop-down list allows you to select the computer, workgroup, or domain from which to choose user accounts, groups, or computers when you assign permissions.

4. In the Name list box, click Users and then click the Add button.

   The Select Users, Computers, Or Groups dialog box displays Computerz\Users in the list box at the bottom of the window.

5. Click OK to return to the News Properties dialog box.

   What are the existing allowed folder permissions?

   _____

   _____

   _____

6. Make sure that Users is selected, and then next to Write, select the Allow check box.

7. Click the Apply button to save your changes.

▶ **To assign permissions to the Creator Owner group for the News folder**

1. In the News Properties dialog box, click the Add button.

   The Select Users, Computers, Or Groups dialog box appears.

2. In the Look In drop-down list at the top of the dialog box, select your computer, Computerz.

3. In the Name list box, select Creator Owner and then click the Add button.

   Creator Owner appears in the list box at the bottom of the dialog box.

4. Click OK to return to the News Properties dialog box.

5. Make sure that Creator Owner is selected. Then next to Full Control, select the Allow check box, and click the Apply button to save your changes.

   Notice that the permissions for Creator Owner show no check boxes selected. To understand why, continue on with the next step.

6. Click the Advanced button to display the additional permissions.

   The Access Control Settings For Public dialog box appears.

7. In the Permission Entries list box, select Creator Owner, if necessary.

Which permissions are assigned to Creator Owner, and where do these permissions apply?

_____

_____

_____

_____

_____

8. Click OK to close the Access Control Settings For News dialog box.

9. Click OK to close the News Properties dialog box.

10. Close Windows Explorer.

► **To test the folder permissions that you assigned for the News folder**

1. Log on to your local computer as User17, and then start Windows Explorer.

2. Expand the News folder.

3. In the News folder, attempt to create a text document named User17.

Were you successful? Why or why not?

_____

_____

4. Attempt to perform the following tasks with the file you just created, and then record those tasks that you are able to complete:

   ■ Open the file.

   ■ Modify the file.

   ■ Delete the file.

_____

_____

_____

5. Close all applications, and then log off your computer.

Exercise 3
Assigning NTFS Permissions

In this exercise, you will assign NTFS permissions to the TechApps, TechApps\FixesDB, TechApps\Troubleshoot, TechTips, and TechTips\OpenDB folders based on the following scenario.

▶ **Scenario**

In the procedure below, to assign NTFS permissions for a folder, you will assign the appropriate permissions to the folders listed in the following table:

Path	User Account or Group	NTFS Permissions
TechApps	Administrators group	Full Control
	Users group	Read & Execute
TechApps\Troubleshoot	Administrators group	Full Control
	Users group	Read & Execute
TechApps\FixesDB	Administrators group	Full Control
	Technicians group	Read & Execute
	Leads group	Read & Execute
	Directors group	Read & Execute
	User21 and User22	Read & Execute and Write
TechTips	Administrators group	Full Control
	Users group	Read & Execute
TechTips\OpenDB	Administrators group	Full Control
	Technicians group	Read & Execute and Write
	Leads group	Read & Execute
	Directors group	Read & Execute

▶ **To remove permissions from the Everyone group**

1. Log on to your local computer as Administrator using a password of "password".

2. Start Windows Explorer, expand Local Disk (C:), right-click the TechTips folder, and then click Properties.

   The TechTips Properties dialog box appears.

3. Click on the Security tab to display the permissions for the TechTips folder.

   Notice that default permissions for a new folder are currently assigned: the Everyone group has the Full Control NTFS permission, and the currently allowed permissions can't be modified.

4. Under Name, ensure that the Everyone group is selected and then click the Remove button.

   A Security message box appears, indicating that you can't remove "Everyone" because the folder is inheriting the permissions for the Everyone group from its parent folder. To change permissions for Everyone, you must first block inheritance.

5. Click OK to close the message box, and then clear the Allow Inheritable Permissions From Parent To Propagate To This Object check box to block permissions.

   A Security dialog box appears, prompting you to copy the previously inherited permissions to the folder or remove all inherited permissions for the folder except those that you explicitly specify.

6. Click the Remove button.

   The Everyone group is deleted.

7. Repeat the procedure above for the TechApps folder.

   Leave the TechApps Properties dialog box open for the next procedure.

▶ **To assign NTFS permissions for a folder**

Note On the Security tab of the TechApps Properties dialog box, if you need to modify the inherited permissions for a user, account, or group, clear the Allow Inheritable Permissions From Parent To Propagate To This Object check box. When prompted to copy or remove inherited permissions, click the Copy button.

1. To add permissions to user accounts or groups for the folder, click the Add button.

Note If the Enter Network Password dialog box appears, click Cancel to close it.

   The Select Users, Computers, Or Groups dialog box appears.

2. Make sure that your computer name appears in the Look In drop-down list at the top of the dialog box.

3. In the Name list box, select the name of the appropriate user account or group, based on the scenario for this exercise, and then click the Add button.

   The user account or group is displayed in the list box at the bottom of the dialog box.

4. Repeat step 4 for each user account or group that is listed for the TechApps folder in the scenario for this exercise.

5. Click OK to return to the Properties dialog box for the TechApps folder.

6. If the Properties dialog box for the TechApps folder contains user accounts and groups that are not listed in the scenario for this exercise, select the user account or group and then click the Remove button.

7. For all user accounts and groups that are listed for the TechApps folder in the scenario for this exercise, in the Name list box, select a user account or group, and then under Permissions, select the Allow check box or the Deny check box next to the appropriate permissions that are listed for the folder in the scenario.

8. Click OK to apply your changes and close the Properties dialog box for the TechApps folder.

9. Repeat this procedure to assign permissions for the TechTips\FixesDB folder, as specified in the scenario for this exercise.

10. Log off your computer.

Exercise 4
Testing NTFS Permissions

In this exercise, you will log on using various user accounts and test NTFS permissions.

▶ **To test permissions for the FixesDB folder while logged on as User17**

1. Log on to your local computer as User17, a member of the Leads group, and then start Windows Explorer.

2. In Windows Explorer, expand the TechApps\FixesDB folder.

3. Attempt to create a text document in the FixesDB folder.

   Were you successful? Why or why not?

   _____

   _____

4. Log off your computer.

▶ **To test permissions for the FixesDB folder while logged on as User21**

1. Log on to your local computer as User21, and then start Windows Explorer.

2. Expand the TechApps\FixesDB folder.

3. Attempt to create a file in the FixesDB folder.

   Were you successful? Why or why not?

   _____

4. Rename the new file User21, and then delete the file.

   Were you successful? Why or why not?

   _____

5. Log off your computer, and log on as Administrator with a password of "password".

6. Assign User21 the NTFS Modify permission for the TechApps\FixesDB folder.

7. Log off your computer, and log on as User21 with a password of User21.

8. Rename the file New Text Document in the TechApps\FixesDB folder, and then delete the file.

   Were you successful? Why or why not?

   _____

   _____

9. Log off your computer.

▶ **To test permissions for the OpenDB folder while logged on as Administrator**

1. Log on to your local computer as Administrator with a password of "password", and then start Windows Explorer.

2. Expand the TechTips\OpenDB folder.

3. Attempt to create a text document in the OpenDB folder, rename the document Admin1, and then delete the document.

   Were you successful? Why or why not?

   _____

   _____

4. Log off your computer.

▶ **To test permissions for the OpenDB folder while logged on as User18**

1. Log on to your local computer as User18, and then start Windows Explorer.

2. Expand the TechTips\OpenDB folder.

3. Attempt to create a text document in the OpenDB folder, rename the document User18, and then delete the document.

   Were you successful? Why or why not?

   _____

   _____

   _____

   _____

4. Log off your computer.

Lab 17: Managing NTFS Permissions

Objectives

After completing this lab, you will be able to

- Assign permissions for a user or group to take ownership of a file or folder.
- Take ownership of a file or folder.
- Understand how copying and moving folders and files affect permissions.
- Apply NTFS folder and file permissions to users and groups.
- Prevent users with Full Control permission for a folder from deleting files in that folder.

Before You Begin

To successfully complete this lab, you must have completed Lab 16, "Planning and Assigning NTFS Permissions," in the *ALS: Microsoft Windows 2000 Professional* Lab Manual.

Estimated time to complete this lab: 30 minutes

Exercise 1
Taking Ownership of a File

In this exercise, you will observe the effects of taking ownership of a file. To do this, you must determine permissions for a file, assign the Take Ownership permission to a user account, and then take ownership of the file as that user.

▶ **To determine the permissions for a file**

1. Log on to your local computer as Administrator using a password of "password".

2. Start Windows Explorer, click Local Disk (C:), and create a text document named Owner.

3. Right-click the Owner text document, and then click Properties.

   The Owner Properties dialog box appears, with the General tab active.

4. Click the Security tab to display the permissions for the Owner file.

   What are the currently allowed permissions for the Owner file?

   _____

   _____

5. Click the Advanced button.

   The Access Control Settings For Owner dialog box appears, with the Permissions tab active.

6. In the Access Control Settings For Owner dialog box, click the Owner tab.

   Who is the current owner of the Owner file?

   _____

▶ **To assign permission to a user to take ownership**

1. In the Access Control Settings For Owner dialog box, click the Permissions tab.

2. Click the Add button.

3. If the Enter Network Password dialog box appears, click Cancel to close the dialog box.

Note Normally in a domain environment, you do not use local user accounts. For this class, we are using local user accounts.

   The Select User, Computer, Or Group dialog box appears.

4. In the Look In drop-down list at the top of the dialog box, ensure that your computer, Computer$z$, is selected.

5. Under Name, click User17 and then click Ok.

   The Permission Entry For Owner dialog box appears.

   Notice that all of the permission entries for User17 are blank.

6. Under Permissions, select the Allow check box next to Take Ownership.

7. Click OK.

   The Access Control Settings For Owner dialog box with the Permissions tab displayed is once again active.

8. Click OK to return to the Owner Properties dialog box.

9. Click OK to apply your changes and close the Owner Properties dialog box.

10. Close all applications, and then log off your computer.

▶ **To take ownership of a file**

1. Log on to your local computer as User17, and then start Windows Explorer.

2. Expand Local Disk (C:).

3. Right-click the Owner text file, and then click Properties.

   The Owner Properties dialog box appears, with the General tab active.

4. Click the Security tab to display the permissions for the Owner file.

   A Security message box appears, indicating that you can view only the current security information for the Owner file.

5. Click OK.

   The Owner Properties dialog box appears, with the Security tab active.

6. Click the Advanced button to display the Access Control Settings For Owner dialog box, and then click the Owner tab.

   Who is the current owner of the Owner file?

   _____

7. Under Change Owner To, select User17 and then click the Apply button.

   Who is the current owner of the Owner file?

   _____

8. Click Cancel to close the Access Control Settings For Owner dialog box.

   The Owner Properties dialog box is displayed once again, with the Security tab active.

▶ **To test permissions for a file as the owner**

1. While you are logged on as User17, assign User17 the Full Control permission for the Owner file and click the Apply button.

2. Clear the Allow Inheritable Permissions From Parent To Propagate To This Object check box.

3. In the Security dialog box, click the Remove button.

4. Click OK to close the Owner Properties dialog box.

5. Delete the Owner file.

Exercise 2
Copying and Moving Folders

In this exercise, you will observe the effects on permissions and ownership when you copy and move folders.

▶ **To create a folder while logged on as a user**

1. While you are logged on as User17, in Windows Explorer, on drive C:, create a folder named Temp1.

   What are the permissions that are assigned to the folder?

   _____

   Who is the current owner of Temp1?

   _____

2. Close all applications, and then log off your computer.

▶ **To create a folder while logged on as Administrator**

1. Log on to your local computer as Administrator with a password of "password".

2. On drive C:, create two folders named Temp2 and Temp3.

   What are the permissions for Temp2 and Temp3?

   _____

   Who is the current owner of the Temp2 and Temp3 folders? Why?

   _____

   _____

3. For both the Temp2 and Temp3 folders, clear the Allow Inheritable Permissions From Parent To Propagate To This Object check box.

4. Click the Remove button to remove the inherited permissions and keep only those explicitly assigned.

5. Assign the following permissions to the Temp2 and Temp3 folders. To select a group, select the group name in the Name list box and then click the Add button.

Note Make sure you select your computer, Computer*z* (where *z* is your student number), when you are adding users.

Folder	Assign These Permissions
Temp2	Administrators: Full Control Users: Read & Execute
Temp3	Backup Operators: Read & Execute Users: Full Control

▶ **To copy a folder to another folder within a Windows 2000 NTFS volume**

1. While you are logged on as Administrator, in Windows Explorer, copy C:\Temp2 to C:\Temp1 by selecting C:\Temp2, holding down the Ctrl key, and then dragging C:\Temp2 to C:\Temp1.

Note Since this is a copy, C:\Temp2 and C:\Temp1\Temp2 should both exist.

2. Select C:\Temp1\Temp2, and then compare the permissions and ownership to those of C:\Temp2.

   Who is the owner of C:\Temp1\Temp2 and what are the permissions? Why?

   _____

   _____

   _____

   _____

   _____

Exercise 3
Deleting a File with All Permissions Denied

In this exercise, you will grant a user Full Control permission to a folder but deny all permissions to a file in the folder. You will then observe what happens when the user attempts to delete that file.

▶ **To assign the Full Control permission for a folder**

1. While logged on as Administrator, use Windows Explorer to expand drive C:, and then create a folder named Fullaccess.

2. Verify that the Everyone group has the Full Control permission for the Fullaccess folder.

▶ **To create a file and deny access to it**

1. In the Fullaccess folder, create a text document named Noaccess.

2. Deny the Everyone group the Full Control permission for the Noaccess file.

   A Security dialog box appears, with the following message:

   ```
   You have denied everyone access to Noaccess. No one will be able to
   access Noaccess and only the owner will be able to change
   permissions.

   Do you wish to continue?
   ```

3. Click the Yes button to apply your changes and close the Security dialog box.

▶ **To view the result of denying access to a file**

1. In Windows Explorer, double-click the Noaccess file in the Fullaccess folder to open the file.

Note When you double-click the Noaccess file, a Microsoft Notepad window appears.

Were you successful? Why or why not?

_____

_____

_____

2. Close Notepad.

3. Click the Start button, point to Programs, point to Accessories, and then click Command Prompt.

4. Type **cd c:\fullaccess**, and press ENTER to change to the Fullaccess folder on drive C.

5. Type **dir**, and then press ENTER.

   Do you see the file Noaccess listed?

   _____

6. Type **del noaccess.txt**, and then press ENTER.

7. Type **dir**, and then press ENTER.

   Do you see the file Noaccess listed?

   _____

   Were you successful in deleting the Noaccess file? Why or why not?

   _____

   _____

   _____

   _____

   How would you prevent users with Full Control permission for a folder from deleting a file in that folder for which they have been denied the Full Control permissions?

   _____

   _____

8. Close Command Prompt and any open windows, and then log off your computer.

Lab 18: Managing Shared Folders

Objectives

After completing this lab, you will be able to

- Share a folder.
- Assign shared folder permissions.
- Connect to a shared folder.
- Combine shared folder permissions and NTFS permissions.
- Connect to a shared folder using the Map Network Drive command.
- Stop the sharing of a folder.

Estimated time to complete this lab: 30 minutes

Exercise 1
Sharing Folders

In this exercise, you will share a folder.

▶   **To share a folder**

1. Log on to the domain as Student$z$ (where z is your student number) with a password of "password".

2. Start Windows Explorer, create a C:\Resources folder, right-click Resources, and then click Properties.

3. In the Resources Properties dialog box, click the Sharing tab.

   Notice that the folder is currently not shared.

4. Select the Share This Folder radio button.

   Notice that Share Name defaults to the name of the folder. If you wanted the share name to be different from the folder's name, you could change it here.

5. In the Comment text box, type **Shared Troubleshooting Resources** and then click OK.

   Notice that Windows Explorer changes the appearance of the Resources folder icon by placing a hand under it to indicate that it is a shared folder.

Exercise 2
Assigning Shared Folder Permissions

In this exercise, you will determine the current permissions for a shared folder and assign shared folder permissions to groups in your domain.

▶   **To determine the current permissions for the Resources shared folder**

1. In Windows Explorer, right-click C:\Resources and then click Properties.

2. In the Resources Properties dialog box, click the Sharing tab and then click the Permissions button.

   The Permissions For Resources dialog box appears.

   Notice that the default permissions for the Resources shared folder is for the Everyone group to have Full Control permissions.

▶   **To remove permissions for a group**

1. Verify that the Everyone group is selected.

2. Click the Remove button.

▶   **To assign Full Control to the Domain Users group**

1. Click the Add button.

   The Select Users, Computers, Or Groups dialog box appears.

2. Ensure that the Corpy domain is displayed in the Look In drop-down list; then in the Name list box, select Domain Users and then click the Add button.

3. Click OK.

   Domain Users is added to the list of names with permissions.

   Which type of access does Windows 2000 assign to Domain Users by default?

   _____

4. In the Permissions list box, under Allow, click the Full Control check box.

   Why did Windows Explorer also select the Change permission for you?

   _____

5. Click OK to close the Permissions For Resources dialog box.

6. Click OK to close the Resources Properties dialog box.

7. Close Windows Explorer.

Exercise 3
Connecting to a Shared Folder

In this exercise, you connect to a shared folder on your partner's computer.

Note You cannot continue with this exercise until your partner has completed Exercise 2.

▶ **To connect to a shared folder by using the Run command**

1. Log on to the Corp$y$ domain as Student$z$ with a password of "password".

Note Replace y with the number your instructor told you to use, and replace z with the student number that your instructor assigned you.

2. Click the Start button, and then click Run.

3. In the Open text box, type **\\Computer**p (where p is the number of your partner's computer) and then click OK.

   The Computer$p$ window appears.

4. Double-click the Resources folder icon to confirm that you can gain access to its contents.

5. Create a text document in the Resources folder on your partner's computer. Name the text document Student$z$ (where z is your student number).

   Were you able to create a text document? Why or why not?

   _____

   _____

6. Close the Resources On Computer$p$ window.

Exercise 4
Combining Shared Folder Permissions and NTFS Permissions

In this exercise, you will set NTFS permissions and test how they combine with the Shared Folder permissions by connecting to a shared folder on your partner's computer.

▶ **To combine NTFS and Shared Folder permissions**

1. In Windows Explorer, right-click C:\Resources on your local computer and then click Properties.

   The Resources Properties dialog box appears.

2. In the Resources Properties dialog box, click the Security tab.

   Notice that the Everyone group has the Full Control NTFS permission assigned by default.

3. Clear the Allow Inheritable Permissions From Parent To Propagate To This Object check box.

   A Security dialog box appears, prompting you to copy the previously inherited permissions to the folder or remove all inherited permissions for the folder except those that you explicitly specify.

4. Click the Copy button.

5. In the Permission list box, clear the Full Control, Modify, and Write check boxes.

6. Click the Apply button, and then click OK to close the Resources Properties dialog box.

Note You cannot continue with this exercise until your partner has completed Steps 1 through 6.

---

7. Click the Start button, and then click Run.

8. In the Open text box, type **\\Computer*p*** (where *p* is the number of your partner's computer) and then click OK.

   The Computer*p* window appears.

9. Double-click Resources to confirm that you can gain access to its contents.

10. Create a text document in Resources on your partner's computer. Name the text document Student*z*2 (where *z* is your student number).

    Were you able to create a text document? Why or why not?

    _____

    _____

    _____

    _____

    _____

11. Double-click the Studentz file to open it, type in some text, and then save the text document.

Were you able to open and read the text document? Were you able to save the changes you made to the file? Why or why not?

_____

_____

_____

_____

_____

_____

_____

12. Close all open windows.

Exercise 5
Connecting to a Shared Folder Using the Map Network Drive Command

In this exercise, you will use the Map Network Drive command to connect to a shared folder on your partner's computer.

▶ **To connect to a shared folder using the Map Network Drive command**

1. Right-click My Network Places, and then click Map Network Drive.

2. In the Map Network Drive wizard, in the Folder text box, type **\\Computer*p*\Resources** (where *p* is the number of your partner's computer).

3. In the Drive drop-down list, select P.

4. Clear the Reconnect At Logon check box.

   You will gain access to the Resources shared folder on your partner's computer in this exercise. Disabling the option to reconnect will ensure that Windows 2000 won't automatically attempt to reconnect to this shared folder later.

5. To complete the connection, click the Finish button.

   The Resources On 'Computer*p*' (P:) window appears.

   How does Windows Explorer indicate that this drive points to a remote shared folder?

   _____

   _____

6. Close the Resources On 'Computer*p*' (P:) window.

▶ **To disconnect from a shared folder on a network drive using Windows Explorer**

1. Start Windows Explorer.

2. Right-click Resources On 'Computer*p*' (P:), and then click Disconnect.

   Windows 2000 removes Resources On 'Computer*p*' (P:) from the Windows Explorer window.

Exercise 6
Stopping the Sharing of a Folder

In this exercise, you will stop sharing a folder.

▶   **To stop sharing a folder**

1. Right-click C:\Resources on your local computer, and then click Properties.

2. In the Resources Properties dialog box, click the Sharing tab.

3. Click Do Not Share This Folder, and then click OK.

   Notice that Windows 2000 no longer displays the hand that identifies a shared folder under the Resources folder. You might need to refresh the screen; if so, press F5.

4. Close all open windows, and log off.

Lab 19: Auditing Resources and Events

Objectives

After completing this lab, you will be able to

- Set up an audit policy.
- Set up account management auditing.
- Set up privilege use auditing.
- Archive the security log and view an archived log.

Estimated time to complete this lab: 25 minutes

Exercise 1
Setting Up an Audit Policy

In this exercise, you will enable auditing on your computer for the selected events listed in the table for this exercise.

▶   **To set up an audit policy**

1. Log on to your local computer as Administrator using a password of "password".

2. Click the Start button, point to Programs, point to Administrative Tools, and then click Local Security Policy.

   The Local Security Settings snap-in appears.

3. In the console tree of the Local Security Settings window, double-click Local Policies and then click Audit Policy.

4. To set the audit policy, in the Details pane, double-click each type of event and then select either the Success check box, the Failure check box, or both for the Audit These Attempts setting under Local Policy Setting, as listed in the following table:

Actions to Audit	Successful	Failed
Audit Account Management	☑	☐
Audit Object Access	☐	☐
Audit Policy Change	☑	☐
Audit Privilege Use	☑	☐

5. Close the Local Security Settings snap-in.

6. Restart your computer.

Exercise 2
Auditing Account Management

In this exercise, you will create a new user account on your local computer, Audituser, to test how Windows 2000 uses the Audit Account Management event in auditing.

▶ **To test the Audit Account Management event**

1. Log on to the Corp*y* domain as Student*z* (where *z* is your student number) using a password of "password".

2. Click the Start button, point to Programs, point to Administrative Tools, and click Computer Management.

3. Under System Tools, double-click Local Users And Groups to expand it.

4. In the console tree, right-click Users and then click New User.

   The New User dialog box appears.

5. In the User Name text box, type **SteveA2**. Do not assign a password, and clear the User Must Change Password At Next Logon check box.

6. Click the Create button to create the user account, and then close the New User dialog box.

7. Close Computer Management.

8. Click the Start button, point to Programs, point to Administrative Tools, and click Event Viewer.

   The Event Viewer snap-in appears.

9. In the console tree of Event Viewer, select Security Log.

   The security log appears in the Details pane of the Event Viewer snap-in. Notice that there are columns in the Details pane indicating the Date, the Time, the Source, the Category, the Event, and the User. You may have to scroll to the right to see all these columns.

10. In the Details pane, double-click the most recent event that shows Account Management in the Category column.

    Notice that user Student*z* has a Success event recorded for Account Management. In the Description box in the Member ID field, it indicates that the Computer*z*\SteveA2 account was created, and in the Caller User Name field, it indicates that Student*z* created the account. You can scroll through the recorded events in Event Viewer by using the up arrow and down arrow buttons.

11. Click Cancel to close the Event Properties dialog box.

12. Minimize Event Viewer.

Exercise 3
Auditing Privilege Use

In this exercise, you change the system time to test how Microsoft Windows 2000 uses the Audit Privilege Use event in auditing. You will then clear the security log to see how Windows 2000 responds to clearing the security log.

▶   **To test auditing of privilege use**

1. Click the Start button, point to Settings, and then click Control Panel.

2. In the Control Panel window, double-click the Date/Time icon.

    The Date/Time Properties dialog box appears.

3. In the Date drop-down list, select yesterday's date and then click OK.

4. Minimize the Control Panel window.

5. Maximize the Event Viewer snap-in.

6. Press F5 to refresh the view and to ensure all recorded events are displayed.

7. Review the list of events displayed in the Details pane.

    Notice the date change in the list of events recorded in the security log. The last entries in the security log have yesterday's date. Notice also the events listed with Privilege Use in the Category column. You can clear the security log to delete all the security log records, including those showing that the date was changed.

8. In the Console tree, ensure that the Security Log is selected.

9. On the Action Menu, click Clear All Events.

    An Event Viewer dialog box appears, asking if you would like to save the security log before it is cleared.

10. Click the Yes button to save the security log.

    The Save "Security Log" As dialog box appears, prompting you for a filename and location.

    What is the default location for saving security logs?

    _____

    _____

11. In the File Name text box, type **SecLog**, make sure that Event Log (*.evt) is selected in the Save As Type drop-down list, and then click the Save button.

    Notice that the security log is not empty.

12. Double-click the event with System Event in the Category column and System in the User column.

    Notice that the first line in the Description box indicates that the audit log was cleared.

13. Click Cancel to close the Event Properties dialog box.

Exercise 4
Archiving the Security Log and Viewing an Archived Log

In this exercise, you will archive the security log file and then open the archived log file.

▶ **To archive the security log file**

1. In the console tree of the Event Viewer snap-in, verify that Security Log is selected.

2. On the Action menu, click Save Log File As.

   The Save "Security Log" As dialog box appears.

3. In the File Name text box, type **SecLog***date*, where *date* is today's date. (For example, if today's date were June 18, 2000, you would type **SecLog61800**.)

4. Ensure that Event Log (*.evt) is selected in the Save As Type drop-down list, and then click the Save button.

▶ **To view an archived security log file**

1. Verify that in the console tree, Security Log is selected.

2. On the Action menu, click Open Log File.

   The Open dialog box appears. Notice that the file you created when you cleared the security log, SecLog.evt, is also one of the files you can view.

3. Select SecLog*date*.

4. In the Log Type list box, select Security and then click Open to open the SecLog*date*.evt file.

   Notice that Saved Security Log is added in the console tree and that the saved SecLog*date*.evt log file opens in the Event Viewer snap-in.

5. Close the Event Viewer snap-in.

6. Log off.

Lab 20: Configuring Account Policies

Objectives

After completing this lab, you will be able to

- Configure minimum password length.
- Configure password history.
- Configure minimum and maximum password age.

Estimated time to complete this lab: 25 minutes

Exercise 1
Configuring Minimum Password Length

In this exercise, you will configure a Password Policy setting, Minimum Password Length, for your computer. Then you will test the password length you configured to confirm that it was set.

▶ **To configure the Minimum Password Length setting**

1. Log on to your local computer as Administrator using a password of "password".

2. Use Microsoft Management Console (MMC) to create a custom console containing the Group Policy snap-in, and save the console with the name Group Policy.

   The Group Policy snap-in appears.

3. In the Group Policy console tree, expand Local Computer Policy and then expand Computer Configuration\Windows Settings\Security Settings\Account Policies.

4. Click Password Policy in the console tree.

5. In the Details pane, right-click Minimum Password Length and then click Security.

   The Local Security Policy Setting dialog box appears. Notice that at the bottom of the dialog box there is the following message:

   ```
   If domain-level policy settings are defined they override local
   policy settings.
   ```

6. Type **7** in the Characters spin box, and then click OK.

7. On the Console menu, click Save and then close the Group Policy snap-in.

▶ **To test the Minimum Password Length setting**

1. Press CTRL+ALT+DELETE, and in the Windows Security dialog box, click Change Password.

2. In the Old Password text box, type **password**, and then in the New Password and Confirm Password text boxes, type **flower**.

   Were you able to change your password to "flower"? Why or why not?

   _____

   _____

3. If you were able to change your password to "flower", change the Administrator password back to "password".

4. Click Cancel to close the Windows Security dialog box.

Note For the purposes of this class, you are going to remove your computer from the domain so that you can use your local security policy settings. You will later rejoin the domain.

▶ **To remove your computer from the domain**

1. Right-click My Computer, and click Properties.

   The System Properties dialog box appears.

2. Click the Network Identification tab.

3. On the Network Identification tab, click the Properties button.

   The Identification Changes dialog box appears. Notice that your computer is currently a member of the corp$y$.corp.com domain (where y is the value your instructor assigned to the domain).

4. In the Member Of group box, select the Workgroup radio button, and then in the Workgroup text box, type **Workgroup** and then click OK.

   After a few seconds, a Network Identification message box appears with the following message:

   ```
   This computer was disjoined from the domain 'CORPy.CORP.COM' but the
   computer account could not be disabled. You should contact your
   network administrator with this information.
   ```

5. Click OK to close the Network Identification message box.

   A Network Identification message box appears welcoming you to the workgroup Workgroup.

6. Click OK to close the second Network Identification message box.

   A third Network Identification message box appears indicating that you must reboot your computer for the changes to take effect.

7. Click OK to close the third Network Identification message box.

8. Click OK to close the System Properties dialog box.

   A System Settings Change message box appears, asking if you want to restart your computer now.

9. Click the Yes button to reboot the system.

▶ **To test the Minimum Password Length setting**

Note Now that your computer is no longer a member of the domain, you will test your local security policy settings.

1. Log on to your local computer as Administrator using a password of "password".

2. Press CTRL+ALT+DELETE, and in the Windows Security dialog box, click the Change Password button.

3. In the Old Password text box, type **password**, and then in the New Password and Confirm Password text boxes, type **flower**.

4. Click OK.

   A Change Password message box appears indicating that your new password must be at least seven characters long, verifying that the Minimum Password Length setting in Password Policy is working.

5. Click OK to close the Change Password message box.

6. Click Cancel to close the Change Password dialog box and leave your password set to 'password'.

7. Click Cancel again to close the Windows Security dialog box.

Exercise 2
Configuring and Testing Additional Account Policies Settings

In this exercise, you will configure and test additional Account Policies settings.

▶ **To configure Account Policies settings**

1. Click the Start button, point to Programs, point to Administrative Tools, and click Group Policy.

2. Use the Group Policy snap-in to configure the following Account Policies settings:

   ■ A user must have at least four different passwords before he or she is able to reuse a previously used password.

   ■ After changing a password, a user must wait 48 hours before changing it again.

   ■ A user must change his or her password every four weeks.

   Which settings did you use for each of the three listed items?

   _____

   _____

   _____

   _____

   _____

   _____

3. Close the Group Policy snap-in, and save the changes.

▶ **To test Account Policies settings**

1. Log on to your local computer as User4 with no password.

Note If you get a Logon Message dialog box indicating that your password will expire in a specified number of days and asking if you want to change it now, click No.

2. Change your password to "flowers".

   Were you successful? Why or why not?

   _____

   _____

3. Change your password to "elephant".

   Were you successful? Why or why not?

   _____

   _____

   _____

4. Close all windows, and log off.

Exercise 3
Configuring Account Lockout Policy

In this exercise, you will configure the Account Lockout Policy settings, and then you will test them to make sure they're set up correctly.

▶   **To configure the Account Lockout Policy settings**

1. Log on to your local computer as Administrator using a password of "password".

2. Click the Start button, point to Programs, point to Administrative Tools, and then click Group Policy.

3. In the Group Policy console tree, expand Local Computer Policy\Computer Configuration\Windows Settings\Security Settings\Account Policies.

4. Click Account Lockout Policy.

5. Use Account Lockout Policy settings to do the following:

   ■ Lock out a user account after four failed logon attempts

   ■ Lock out user accounts until the administrator unlocks them

   Which Account Lockout Policy settings did you use for each of the two conditions?

   _____

   _____

   _____

   _____

   _____

   _____

6. Close the Group Policy snap-in, and then click the Yes button to save the settings.

7. Log off as Administrator.

▶   **To test the Account Lockout Policy settings**

1. Try to log on to your local computer as User4 with a password of "papers". Try this four times.

2. Try to log on a fifth time as User4 with a password of "papers".

   A Logon Message message box appears, indicating that the account is locked out.

3. Click OK, and then log off.

▶   **To unlock the User4 user account**

1. Log on to your local computer as Administrator with a password of "password".

2. Click the Start button, point to Programs, point to Administrative Tools, and then click Computer Management.

3. In the Computer Management console tree, double-click Local Users And Groups and then click Users.

4. In the Details pane, right-click User4 and then click Properties.

   In the User4 Properties dialog box, notice that Account Is Locked Out is not grayed out and that its check box is selected.

5. Clear the Account Is Locked Out check box, and then click OK.

   The User4 account is now unlocked.

6. In the Details pane, right-click User4 and then click Properties.

   In the User4 Properties dialog box, notice that User4 is no longer locked out and that the option is now grayed out.

7. Log on to your local computer as User4 with a password of "flowers".

Lab 21: Configuring Security Settings

Objectives

After completing this lab, you will be able to

- Configure security settings.

Estimated time to complete this lab: 15 minutes

Exercise 1
Configuring Security Settings

In this exercise, you will configure Security Options on your computer. You will configure the Security Options to force users to log on in order to be able to shut down the computer, to force users to press CTRL+ALT+DELETE to log on to the computer, and to prevent Microsoft Windows 2000 from displaying the user account last logged on the computer in the Windows Security dialog box. Then you will test these security settings to confirm that you configured them correctly.

▶   **To configure Security Options settings**

1. Log on to your local computer as Administrator using a password of "password".

2. Click the Start button, point to Programs, point to Administrative Tools, and then click Group Policy.

3. In the Group Policy console tree, expand Local Computer Policy\Computer Configuration\Windows Settings\Security Settings\Local Policies.

4. Click Security Options.

5. Configure your computer so that the following conditions are true:

   ▪ Users must log on to shut down the computer.

   ▪ Users must press CTRL+ALT+DELETE to log on to the computer.

   ▪ Windows 2000 will not display in the Windows Security dialog box the user account last logged on to the computer.

   Which Security Option did you use for each of these three conditions?

   _____

   _____

   _____

   _____

   _____

   _____

   _____

6. Close the Group Policy Local window, and then click the Yes button to save the settings.

7. Log off.

   Notice that you are prompted to press CTRL+ALT+DELETE to log on.

8. Press CTRL+ALT+DELETE.

Notice that the Log On To Windows dialog box appears with the User Name text box blank and that the Shutdown button is dimmed. (Click the Options button if you cannot see the Shutdown button.)

Note You will now add your computer back to the domain.

▶ **To add your computer to the domain**

1. Log on to the computer as Administrator with a password of "password".

2. Right-click My Computer, and click Properties.

The System Properties dialog box appears.

3. Click the Network Identification tab.

4. On the Network Identification tab, click the Properties button.

The Identification Changes dialog box appears. Notice that your computer is currently a member of the Workgroup workgroup.

5. In the Member Of group box, select the Domain radio button, and in the Domain text box, type **corpy.corp.com** and then click OK.

Note Remember to replace the *y* in corpy.corp.com with the correct number for your domain. If you do not remember the number, ask your instructor.

A Domain Username And Password dialog box appears, prompting you for a username and password that can add a computer to the domain.

6. In the Name text box, type **Studentz** (where *z* is your student number), and in the Password text box, type **password** and then click OK.

A Network Identification message box appears welcoming you to the Corpy.Corp.Com domain.

7. Click OK to close the Network Identification message box.

A second Network Identification message box appears, indicating that you must reboot your computer for the changes to take effect.

8. Click OK to close this Network Identification message box.

9. Click OK to close the System Properties dialog box.

A System Settings Change dialog box appears, asking if you want to reboot now.

10. Click the Yes button to reboot the system.

Lab 22: Managing NTFS Compression

Objectives

After completing this lab, you will be able to

- Compress folders and files in an NTFS partition.
- Display compressed folders and files in a different color.
- Uncompress files and folders.

Before You Begin

Before beginning this lab, you must have created the folder structure outlined at the beginning of Lab 16.

Estimated time to complete this lab: 20 minutes

Exercise 1
Compressing Files in an NTFS Partition

In this exercise, you will use Windows Explorer to compress files and folders in order to make more disk space available on your NTFS partition.

▶ **To view the capacity of and the free space for drive C**

1. Log on to your local computer as Administrator using a password of "password", and then start Windows Explorer.

2. Right-click drive C, and then click Properties.

   The Local Disk (C:) Properties dialog box appears, with the General tab active.

   What is the capacity of drive C?

   _____

   What is the free space on drive C?

   _____

3. Click Cancel to close the Local Disk (C:) Properties dialog box and return to Windows Explorer.

▶ **To compress a folder**

1. In Windows Explorer, expand Local Disk (C:).

2. Right-click the C:\TechTips folder, and then click Properties.

   The TechTips Properties dialog box appears, with the General tab active.

3. On the General tab, click the Advanced button.

   The Advanced Attributes dialog box appears.

4. Select the Encrypt Contents To Secure Data check box.

5. Select the Compress Contents To Save Disk Space check box.

   Notice that the system automatically removes the check mark from the Encrypt Contents To Secure Data check box.

6. Click OK to return to the TechTips Properties dialog box.

7. Click the Apply button to apply your settings.

   The Confirm Attribute Changes dialog box appears, prompting you to specify whether to compress only this folder or this folder, all subfolders, and all files.

8. Ensure that the default option Apply Changes To This Folder Only is selected, and then click OK.

Note If you had chosen the Apply Changes To This Folder, Subfolders And Files option, an Applying Attributes message box would appear, indicating the progress of the operation and the paths and names of folders and files as they are compressed.

---

9. Click OK to close the TechTips Properties dialog box.

Exercise 2
Displaying Compressed Files in a Different Color

In this exercise, you will use Windows Explorer to display compressed files and folders in a different color.

▶ **To display compressed files and folders with an alternate color**

1. In Windows Explorer, click Local Disk (C:) and, on the Tools menu, click Folder Options.

   The Folder Options dialog box appears, with the General tab active.

2. Click on the View tab.

   Answer the following questions:

   Which of the Advanced Setting options allows you to have Windows 2000 display all file extensions in Windows Explorer?

   _____

   _____

   _____

   How would you remove the My Documents icon from your desktop?

   _____

   _____

   _____

3. In the Advanced Settings list, select the Display Compressed Files And Folders With Alternate Color check box.

   Notice in the Folder Views group box, you can click the Like Current Folder button to make all the folders match the settings you have configured on the selected folder.

4. Click OK to apply your changes.

   Windows Explorer displays the names of compressed files and folders in blue.

Exercise 3
Copying and Moving Compressed Files

In this exercise, you will learn the effects that copying and moving files have on compressed files.

▶   **To create a compressed file**

1. In Windows Explorer, click the TechTips folder.

2. On the File menu, click New and then click Text Document.

3. Type **Comp1**, and then press ENTER.

    How can you verify that Comp1 is compressed?

    _____

    _____

▶   **To copy a compressed file to an uncompressed folder**

1. Copy Comp1 to the TechTips\OpenDB folder.

Note Make sure that you copy (hold down the CTRL key while you drag the file) and do not move the file.

2. Examine the properties for Comp1 in the OpenDB folder.

    Is the TechTips\OpenDB\Comp1 file compressed or uncompressed? Why?

    _____

    _____

    _____

▶   **To move a compressed file to an uncompressed folder**

1. Examine the properties of the Comp1 file in the TechTips\OpenDB folder.

    Is TechTips\OpenDB\Comp1 compressed or uncompressed?

    _____

2. Move TechTips\Comp1 to the TechTips\OpenDB folder. When the Confirm File Replace dialog box appears, asking you whether or not you want to re-place the file, click the Yes button.

3. Examine the properties of TechTips\OpenDB\Comp1.

    Is TechTips\OpenDB\Comp1 compressed or uncompressed? Why?

    _____

    _____

Exercise 4
Copying and Moving Uncompressed Files

In this exercise, you will learn the effects that copying and moving files have on uncompressed files.

► **To create an uncompressed file**

1. In Windows Explorer, click the TechTips\OpenDB folder.

2. On the File menu, click New and then click Text Document.

3. Type **Uncomp1**, and then press ENTER.

   How can you verify that Uncomp1 is not compressed?

   _____

   _____

► **To copy an uncompressed file to a compressed folder**

1. Copy the TechTips\OpenDB\Uncomp1 file to the TechTips folder.

Note Make sure that you copy (hold down the CTRL key while you drag the file) and do not move the file.

2. Examine the properties for the Uncomp1 file in the TechTips folder.

   Is the TechTips\Uncomp1 file compressed or uncompressed? Why?

   _____

   _____

   _____

► **To move an uncompressed file to a compressed folder**

1. Examine the properties of the Uncomp1 file in the TechTips\OpenDB folder.

   Is TechTips\OpenDB\Uncomp1 compressed or uncompressed?

   _____

2. Move the TechTips\OpenDB\Uncomp1 file to the TechTips folder. When the Confirm File Replace dialog box appears, asking you whether or not you want to replace the file, click the Yes button.

3. Examine the properties of TechTips\Uncomp1.

   Is TechTips\Uncomp1 compressed or uncompressed? Why?

   _____

   _____

Exercise 5
Uncompressing Files and Folders

In this exercise, you will use Windows Explorer to uncompress a file and a folder.

▶ **To uncompress a file**

1. Right-click the TechTips\OpenDB\Comp1 file, and then click Properties.

   The Comp1 Properties dialog box appears, with the General tab active.

2. On the General tab, click the Advanced button.

   The Advanced Attributes dialog box appears.

3. Clear the Compress Contents To Save Disk Space check box, and then click OK to apply your settings.

4. Click OK to close the TechTips\OpenDB\Comp1 Properties dialog box.

▶ **To uncompress a folder**

1. In Windows Explorer, select the TechTips folder, right-click TechTips, and then click Properties.

   The TechTips Properties dialog box appears, with the General tab active.

2. On the General tab, click the Advanced button.

   The Advanced Attributes dialog box appears.

3. Clear the Compress Contents To Save Disk Space check box, and then click OK to apply your settings.

   What indication do you have that the TechTips folder is no longer compressed?

   _____

   _____

Lab 23: Enabling and Disabling Disk Quotas

Objectives

After completing this lab, you will be able to

- Configure default quota management settings.
- Configure custom quota settings for a user account.
- Disable quota management.

Estimated time to complete this lab: 15 minutes

Note If you didn't install Windows 2000 Professional on drive C, substitute the NTFS partition on which you did install Windows 2000 Professional whenever drive C is referred to in this lab.

Exercise 1
Configuring and Testing Quota Management Settings

In this exercise, you will configure default quota management settings for drive C to limit the data that users can store on the volume. You will then configure custom quota settings for a user account. Finally, you will test the quota settings for a user.

▶ **To configure default quota management settings**

1. Log on to your local computer as Administrator using a password of "password".

2. Create a user account on your local computer, User5, and assign it the password of "password". Clear the User Must Change Password At Next Logon check box.

Note Refer to Chapter 10 in the *ALS: Microsoft Windows 2000 Professional* textbook if you need help setting up a user account on your local computer.

3. In Window Explorer, right-click drive C and then click Properties.

   The Local Disk (C:) Properties dialog box appears, with the General tab active.

4. Click the Quota tab.

   Notice that disk quotas are disabled by default.

5. On the Quota tab, select the Enable Quota Management check box.

   What is the default disk space limit for new users?

   _____

6. Select the Deny Disk Space To Users Exceeding Quota Limit check box.

7. Select the Limit Disk Space To radio button.

8. Type **10** in the Limit Disk Space To text box, and then type **6** in the Set Warning Level To text box.

   Notice that the default unit size is KB.

9. Change the unit size of both text boxes to MB, and then click the Apply button.

   A Disk Quota message box appears, warning you that the volume will be rescanned to update disk usage statistics if you enable quotas.

10. Click OK to enable disk quotas.

▶ **To configure quota management settings for a user**

1. On the Quota tab of the Local Disk (C:) Properties dialog box, click the Quota Entries button.

The Quota Entries For Local Disk (C:) window appears. Are any user accounts listed? Why or why not?

_____

_____

2. On the Quota menu, click New Quota Entry.

   The Enter Network Password dialog box appears.

3. Click Cancel.

   The Select Users dialog box appears.

4. In the Look In drop-down list, select Computer*z* (where *z* is your student number).

5. At the top of the Select Users dialog box, under Name, select User5 and then click the Add button.

   The username appears in the list box at the bottom of the Select Users dialog box.

6. Click OK.

   The Add New Quota Entry dialog box appears. What are the default settings for User5?

_____

_____

7. Increase the amount of data that User5 can store on drive C by changing the Limit Disk Space To text box to 20 MB, and the Set Warning Level To text box to 16 MB.

8. Click OK to return to the Quota Entries For Local Disk (C:) window.

9. Close the Quota Entries For Local Disk (C:) window.

10. Click OK to close the Local Disk (C:) Properties dialog box.

11. Log off.

▶   **To test quota management settings**

   1. Log on to your local computer as User5 with a password of "password".

   2. Start Windows Explorer, and create a User5 folder on drive C.

   3. Copy the files in the C:\Winnt\System32 folder to the User5 folder.

Note Remember to hold the CTRL key down when you drag the folder.

Windows 2000 Professional begins copying the files from the Winnt folder to the User5 folder on drive C. After copying several files, however, an Error Copying File Or Folder message box appears, indicating that there isn't enough room on the disk.

Why did you get the error message?

_____

_____

4. Click OK to close the message box.

5. Right-click the User5 folder, and then click Properties.

   Notice that the Size On Disk value is slightly less than your quota limit of 20 MB.

6. Close all open windows, and log off.

Exercise 2
Disabling Quota Management

In this exercise, you will disable quota management settings for drive C.

▶   **To disable default quota management settings for drive C**

1. Log on to your local computer as Administrator using a password of "password".

2. Start Windows Explorer, and delete the User5 folder.

3. Right-click drive C, and then click Properties.

   The Local Disk (C:) Properties dialog box appears, with the General tab active.

4. Click the Quota tab.

5. On the Quota tab, clear the Enable Quota Management check box.

   Notice that quota settings for drive C are no longer available.

6. Click the Apply button.

   A Disk Quota message box appears, warning you that if you disable quotas, the volume will be rescanned if you enable them later.

7. Click OK to close the Disk Quota message box.

8. Click OK to close the Local Disk (C:) Properties dialog box.

9. Close all windows, and log off.

Lab 24: Encrypting and Decrypting Files

Objectives

After completing this lab, you will be able to

- Encrypt and decrypt folders and files.

Estimated time to complete this lab: 15 minutes

Note If you didn't install Windows 2000 Professional on drive C, substitute the NTFS partition on which you did install Windows 2000 Professional whenever drive C is referred to in these exercises.

Exercise 1
Encrypting Files

In this exercise, you will encrypt a folder and its files.

▶ **To encrypt a file**

1. Log on to your local computer as Administrator using a password of "password".

2. Start Windows Explorer, and in the root of drive C, create the folder Secret, then in the folder Secret, create a text file named File1.

3. Right-click File1, and click Properties.

   The File1 Properties dialog box appears, with the General tab active.

4. Click the Advanced button.

   The Advanced Attributes dialog box appears.

5. Select the Encrypt Contents To Secure Data check box, and then click OK to save your settings and close the Advanced Attributes dialog box.

6. Click OK to close the File1 Properties dialog box.

   An Encryption Warning dialog box informs you that you are about to encrypt a file that isn't in an encrypted folder. Notice that the default is to encrypt the folder and file, but you can also choose to encrypt only the file.

7. Ensure that the Encrypt The File And The Parent Folder option is selected, and then click OK.

   You have just encrypted both File1 and the parent folder Secret.

Note If you had decided to encrypt the folder Secret first instead of starting with the file File1, in the Secret Properties dialog box, you would click the Advanced button. In the Advanced Attributes dialog box, you would select Encrypt Contents To Secure Data and then click OK. When you click OK on the Secret Properties dialog box, a Confirm Attribute Changes dialog box would appear and you would have two choices: Apply Changes To This Folder Only or Apply Changes To This Folder, Subfolders, And Files.

▶ **To verify that the folder's content is encrypted**

1. In the Secret folder, right-click File1 and click Properties.

   The File1 Properties dialog box appears.

2. Click the Advanced button.

   The Advanced Attributes dialog box appears. Notice that the Encrypt Contents To Secure Data check box is selected.

3. Click OK to close the Advanced Attributes dialog box.

4. Click OK to close the File1 Properties dialog box.

5. Close all windows, and log off.

Exercise 2
Testing the Encrypted Files

In this exercise, you will log on as User5 and then attempt to open an encrypted file. You will then try to disable encryption on the encrypted file.

▶ **To test an encrypted file**

1. Log on to your local computer as User5 with a password of "password".
2. Start Windows Explorer, and in the Secret folder, open File1.

   What happens?

   _____

3. Click OK to close the message box, and then close Microsoft Notepad.

▶ **To attempt to disable the encryption**

1. Right-click File1, and then click Properties.
2. Click the Advanced button.
3. Clear the Encrypt Contents To Secure Data check box, and then click OK.
4. Click OK to close the File1 Properties dialog box.

   An Error Applying Attributes message box appears and informs you that access to the file is denied.

5. Click Cancel.
6. Close all open windows and dialog boxes.
7. Log off.

Exercise 3
Decrypting Folders and Files

In this exercise, you will decrypt the folder and file that you previously encrypted.

▶   **To decrypt a file**

1. Log on to your local computer as Administrator with a password of "password".

2. Start Windows Explorer.

3. Right-click Secret\File1, and then click Properties.

   The File1 Properties dialog box appears.

4. Click the Advanced button.

   The Advanced Attributes dialog box appears.

5. Clear the Encrypt Contents To Secure Data check box, and then click OK.

6. Click OK to close the File1 Properties dialog box.

7. Close Windows Explorer.

Lab 25: Defragmenting a Hard Disk

Objectives

After completing this lab, you will be able to

- Analyze a hard disk to see if it needs to be defragmented.
- Defragment a hard disk.

Estimated time to complete this lab: 15 minutes

Note If you didn't install Windows 2000 Professional on drive C, substitute the NTFS partition on which you did install Windows 2000 Professional whenever drive C is referred to in this lab.

Exercise 1
Analyzing and Defragmenting a Hard Disk

In this exercise, you will analyze your hard disk to determine if it needs to be defragmented. Then you will defragment your hard disk.

▶ **To analyze a hard disk**

1. Log on to your local computer as Administrator with a password of "password".

2. Click the Start button, point to Programs, point to Accessories, point to System Tools, and then click Disk Defragmenter.

   The Disk Defragmenter window appears. Notice that you can select the volume you would like to defragment and that the Analyze button and Defragment button are active.

3. Ensure that Volume (C:) is selected, and then click the Analyze button.

   Disk Defragmenter begins to analyze volume C for fragmentation.

   An Analysis Complete dialog box appears.

Note Your student computers should not be very fragmented, so you will get a message indicating that your volume does not need to be defragmented. You can still defragment the volume.

---

4. Click the Defragment button.

   Disk Defragmenter begins to defragment your volume. The length of time it runs will depend on how much fragmentation there is on the volume you have selected.

   A Defragmentation Complete message box appears.

5. Click the View Report button.

   The Defragmentation Report dialog box appears.

   Notice that under Volume Information, the report shows the Volume Size, the Cluster Size, the Used Space and Free Space, and the Percent Free Space. Other lists of information located under Volume Information include Volume Fragmentation, File Fragmentation, PageFile Fragmentation, Directory Fragmentation, and Master File Table (MFT) Fragmentation.

   Notice under Files That Did Not Defragment, columns list the file names, file sizes, and number of fragments of any files that were not defragmented.

6. Click the Save As button to save the report.

   The Save Defragmentation Report dialog box appears. Notice the default name of the report is VolumeC and that it is a text file stored in the My Documents folder.

7. Click the Save button.

   The report is saved, and the Save Defragmentation Report dialog box closes.

8. Click the Close button to close the Defragmentation Report dialog box.

9. Close Disk Defragmenter.

Lab 26: Backing Up Files

Objectives

After completing this lab, you will be able to

- Use Microsoft Windows Backup to back up folders and files.
- View backup reports.
- Use Task Scheduler to create and run an unattended backup.

Note You do not have to have a tape drive attached to your computer to complete this lab.

Estimated time to complete this lab: 25 minutes

Exercise 1
Starting a Backup Job

In this exercise, you start Windows Backup and use the Backup wizard to back up files to your hard disk.

▶ **To back up files by using the Backup wizard**

1. Log on to your local computer as Administrator using a password of "password".

2. Click the Start button, point to Programs, point to Accessories, point to System Tools, and then click Backup.

   The Backup – [Untitled] dialog box appears.

3. On the Welcome tab, click the Backup Wizard button.

   The Backup wizard starts and displays the Welcome To The Windows 2000 Backup And Recovery Tools page.

4. Click Next to continue creating the backup job.

   The What To Back Up page appears, prompting you to choose the scope of the backup job.

5. Select the Back Up Selected Files, Drives, Or Network Data radio button, and then click Next to continue.

   The Items To Back Up page appears, prompting you to select the local and network drives, folders, and files to be backed up.

6. Expand My Computer, expand drive C, and then click C.

Caution Do *not* select drive C. Make sure that the check box in front of drive C is cleared.

7. In the Details pane, select the Boot.ini check box.

Note Boot.ini is one of the boot files for Windows 2000. You will learn more about the Boot.ini file in Chapter 22, "The Windows 2000 Boot Process" in the *ALS: Microsoft Windows 2000 Professional* textbook.

8. Click Next to continue.

   The Where To Store The Backup page appears.

Note If no tape drive is connected to your computer, File will be the only backup media type that is available.

9. In the Backup Media Or File Name text box, type **c:\ backup1.bkf** and then click Next.

Note You wouldn't normally back up files from a drive to a file on that same drive, as you are doing in this exercise. You would normally back up data to a tape or to a file stored on another hard disk, removable disks (such as Iomega Zip and Jaz drives), or recordable compact discs or optical drives.

The Completing The Backup Wizard page appears, prompting you either to finish the wizard and begin the backup job or to specify advanced options.

10. Click the Advanced button to specify additional backup options.

The Type Of Backup page appears, prompting you to select a backup type for this backup job.

11. Verify that Normal is selected in the Select The Type Of Backup Operation To Perform drop-down list.

12. Make sure that the Backup Migrated Remote Storage Data check box is cleared, and then click Next.

The How To Back Up page appears, prompting you to specify whether or not to verify the backed up data after the backup job.

13. Select the Verify Data After Backup check box, and then click Next.

The Media Options page appears, prompting you to specify whether to append this backup job to existing media or overwrite existing backup data on the destination media.

14. Select the Replace The Data On The Media With This Backup radio button.

When is it appropriate to select the check box labeled Allow Only The Owner And The Administrator Access To The Backup Data And To Any Backups Appended To This Media?

---

15. Make sure that the Allow Only The Owner And The Administrator Access To The Backup Data And To Any Backups Appended To This Media check box is cleared, and then click Next.

The Backup Label page appears, prompting you to supply a label for the backup job and a label for the backup media.

Notice that the Backup wizard generates a backup label and a media label by using the current date and time.

16. Press the TAB key to accept the default backup label and to move to the Media Label text box.

17. In the Media Label text box, type **Boot.ini File For Computer**z (where z is your student number) and then click Next.

    The When To Backup page appears, prompting you to choose whether to run the backup job now or to schedule it for later.

18. Make sure that the Now radio button is selected, and then click Next.

    The Completing The Backup Wizard page appears, which lists the options and settings that you selected for this backup job.

19. Click the Finish button to start the backup job.

    A Selection Information message box appears briefly, indicating the estimated amount of data for, and the time to complete, the backup job.

    The Backup Progress dialog box then appears, providing the status of the backup operation, statistics on estimated and actual amount of data being processed, the time that has elapsed, and the estimated time that remains for the backup operation.

▶   **To view a backup report**

1. When the Backup Progress dialog box indicates that the backup is complete, click the Report button.

   Microsoft Notepad starts, displaying the backup report. Notice that the backup report contains key details about the backup operation, such as the time that it started and how many files were backed up.

2. Examine the report, and when you are finished, close Notepad.

3. Close the Backup Progress dialog box.

   The Backup window remains open, with the Welcome tab active.

Exercise 2
Creating and Running an Unattended Backup Job

In this exercise, you create a backup job to perform a backup operation at a later time by using Task Scheduler.

▶   **To create a scheduled backup job**

1. On the Welcome tab, click the Backup Wizard button.

   The Welcome To The Windows 2000 Backup and Recovery Tools page appears.

2. Click Next to continue creating the backup job.

   The What To Back Up page appears, prompting you to choose the scope of the backup job.

3. Select the Back Up Selected Files, Drives, Or Network Data radio button, and then click Next to continue.

   The Items To Back Up page appears, prompting you to select the local and network drives, folders, and files to be backed up.

4. Expand My Computer, expand drive C, and then select the System Volume Information folder check box.

5. Click Next to continue.

   The Where To Store The Backup page appears, prompting you to select the destination for your backup data.

6. In the Backup Media Or File Name text box, type **c:\backup2.bkf** and then click Next.

   The Completing The Backup Wizard page appears.

7. Click the Advanced button to specify additional backup options.

   The Type Of Backup page appears, prompting you to select a backup type for this backup job.

8. Make sure that Normal is selected in the Select The Type Of Backup Operation To Perform drop-down list, and then click Next.

   The How To Back Up page appears, prompting you to specify whether or not to verify the backed up data after the backup job is completed.

9. Select the Verify Data After Backup check box, and then click Next.

   The Media Options page appears, prompting you to specify whether to append this backup job to existing media or to overwrite existing backup data on the destination media.

10. Select the Replace The Data On The Media With This Backup radio button.

11. Make sure the check box labeled Allow Only The Owner And The Administrator Access To The Backup Data And To Any Backups Appended To This Media is cleared, and then click Next.

    The Backup Label page appears, prompting you to supply a label for the backup job and a label for the backup media.

12. In the Media Label text box, type **Backup File 2 For Computer**z (where z is your student number) and then click Next.

    The When To Back Up page appears, prompting you to choose whether to run the backup job now or to schedule it for later.

13. Select the Later radio button.

Note If the Task Scheduler service isn't set to start automatically, you will see a dialog box asking if you want to start the Task Scheduler. Click OK.

The Set Account Information dialog box appears, prompting you for the password for the Administrator account on your local computer.

Note Because the Task Scheduler service automatically runs applications within the security context of a valid user for the computer or domain, you are prompted for the name and password with which the scheduled backup job will run. For scheduled backup jobs, you should supply a user account that is a member of the Backup Operators group with permission to gain access to all of the folders and files to be backed up. For purposes of this lab, you will use the Administrator account to run the scheduled backup job.

---

14. Make sure that Computerz\Administrator (where z is your student number) appears in the Run As text box, and then type **password** in the Password and the Confirm Password text boxes.

15. Click OK.

16. In the Job Name text box, type **Computerz Backup** (where z is your student number) and then click the Set Schedule button.

    The Schedule Job dialog box appears, prompting you to select the start time and schedule options for the backup job.

17. In the Schedule Task drop-down list, select Once, and in the Start Time spin box, enter a time three minutes from the present time and then click OK.

    The When To Back Up page remains displayed along with the scheduled backup job information.

18. Click Next to continue.

    The Completing The Backup Wizard page appears, displaying the options and settings that you selected for this backup job.

19. Click the Finish button to start the backup job.

   The Backup window remains open, with the Welcome tab active.

20. Close the Backup window.

   When the time for the backup job is reached, Windows Backup starts and performs the requested backup operation.

▶   **To verify that the backup job was performed**

1. Start Windows Explorer, and click drive C.

2. Look for the Backup2.bkf file.

   Does the Backup2.bkf file exist?

Lab 27: Restoring Files

Objectives

After completing this lab, you will be able to

- Use Windows Backup to restore files and folders.

Before You Begin

To complete this lab, you must have completed the exercises in the previous lab, or you must have some files you have backed up using Ntbackup that you can restore.

Estimated time to complete this lab: 15 minutes

Exercise 1
Restoring a File

In this exercise, you will restore a file from a previous backup.

▶ **To restore files from a previous backup**

1. Click the Start button, point to Programs, point to Accessories, point to System Tools, and then click Backup.

   The Backup – [Untitled] dialog box appears.

2. In Windows Backup, on the Welcome tab, click the Restore Wizard button.

   The Restore wizard starts and displays the Welcome To The Restore Wizard page.

3. Click Next to continue.

   The What To Restore page appears, prompting you to select the backup media from which you want to restore files.

4. In the What To Restore list box, expand the File node.

   Notice that the Boot.ini File For Computer$z$ and Backup File 2 For Computer$z$ (where z is your student number) are listed.

5. Expand Backup File 2 For Computer$z$.

   Notice that drive C appears under Backup File 2 For Computer$z$.

6. Expand drive C.

   The Backup File Name dialog box appears.

7. In the Catalog Backup File text box, make sure it says C:\Backup2.bkf and then click OK.

   The Operation Status dialog box appears briefly and then closes.

8. Select the System Volume Information check box in either the Tree pane or the Display pane, and then click Next.

   The Completing The Restore Wizard page appears.

9. Click the Advanced button.

   The Where To Restore page appears.

10. In the Restore Files To drop-down list, select Alternate Location.

    The Restore wizard displays the Alternate Location text box.

11. In the Alternate Location text box, type **C:\Restored Data** and then click Next.

    The How To Restore page appears, prompting you to specify how to process duplicate files during the restore job.

12. Make sure that the Do Not Replace The File On My Disk (Recommended) radio button is selected, and then click Next.

    The Advanced Restore Options page appears, prompting you to select security options for the restore job.

13. Make sure that all check boxes are cleared, and then click Next.

    The Completing The Restore Wizard page appears, displaying a summary of the restore options that you selected.

14. Click the Finish button to begin the restore process.

    The Enter Backup File Name dialog box appears, prompting you to supply or verify the name of the backup file that contains the folders and files to be restored.

15. Verify that the file Backup2.bkf is entered in the Restore From Backup File text box, and then click OK.

    A Selection Information message box appears, indicating the estimated amount of data for, and the time to complete, the restore job. (This message box will appear very briefly since you are restoring a single file.)

    The Restore Progress dialog box then appears, providing the status of the restore operation, statistics on estimated and actual amount of data that is being processed, the time that has elapsed, and the estimated time that remains for the restore operation.

▶   **To view a restore report**

1. When the Restore Progress dialog box indicates that the restore is complete, click the Report button.

    Notepad starts, displaying the report. Notice that the details about the restore operation are appended to the previous backup log. This provides a centralized location to view all status information for backup and restore operations.

2. Examine the report, and then close Notepad.

3. Close the Restore Progress dialog box.

    The Backup window remains open, with the Welcome tab active.

▶   **To verify that the data was restored**

1. Start Windows Explorer, and expand drive C.

   Does the Restored Data folder exist?

   _____

   What are the contents of the Restored Data folder?

   _____

Note If the Restored Data folder appears to be empty, ensure that the Restored Data folder is selected, and then on the Tools menu, click Folder Options. On the View tab of the Folder Options dialog box, select the Show Hidden Files And Folders check box and clear the Hide Protected Operating System Files (Recommended) check box. When you are prompted to confirm this action, click the Yes button. Click the Apply button, and then verify that the System Volume Information folder appears in the Restored Data folder.

---

2. Close Windows Explorer, close the Backup window, and then log off.

Lab 28: Managing Shared Folders

Objectives

After completing this lab, you will be able to

- View the shared folders on your computer.
- View the open files on your computer.
- Disconnect all users from open files on your computer.

Estimated time to complete this lab: 15 minutes

Note You will be working in pairs in this lab. One of you will be Partner A, and one of you will be Partner B. Not all the procedures will be completed by both partners.

Exercise 1
Viewing and Creating Shared Folders

In this exercise, you will connect to a shared folder on a network drive.

Note Both partners should complete this exercise.

▶   **To view the shared folders on your computer**

1. Log on to your local computer as Administrator using a password of "password".

2. Click the Start button, point to Programs, point to Administrative Tools, and then click Computer Management.

3. In the console tree of Computer Management, expand System Tools and then expand Shared Folders.

4. In the console tree, under Shared Folders, click Shares.

   Notice that the Details pane shows a list of the existing shared folders on your computer.

▶   **To create a shared folder on your computer Using Windows Explorer**

1. Minimize the Computer Management window and start Windows Explorer.

2. In the C:\ folder, create a folder and name it Lab28. Share this folder as Lab28, and in the Lab28 folder, create a text file and name it OpenTest.

3. Open the text file OpenTest, and type in the following: **This file is to be used with Lab 28.**

4. Save the changes to the OpenTest file.

5. Close the OpenTest file, and then minimize the Windows Explorer window.

Exercise 2
Connecting to a Shared Folder

In this exercise, you will connect to a shared folder on a network drive.

Note Only Partner A should complete this exercise.

▶ **To connect to a shared folder by using the Run command**

1. Log on to the Corp*y* domain as Student*z* with a password of "password".

Important Replace the *y* in Corp*y* with the number your instructor tells you to use and replace the *z* in Student*z* with your student number.

2. Click the Start button, and then click Run.

   The Run dialog box appears.

3. In the Open combo box, type **\\Computer*p*** and then click OK.

Important Be sure you replace the *p* in Computer*p* with your partner's student number.

   The Computer*p* window appears.

4. Double-click the Lab30 folder to confirm that you can gain access to its contents.

5. Double-click OpenTest to open it.

   Leave the OpenTest file open.

Exercise 3
Viewing the Open Files on Your Computer

In this exercise, you will view the open files on your computer.

Note Only Partner B should complete this exercise; Partner A will be an observer.

▶ **To view the open files on your computer**

1. Maximize the Computer Management window.

2. In the console tree, select Open Files under Shared Folders.

   In the Details pane, in the Open File column, what is listed?

Exercise 4
Disconnecting All Users from Open Files on Your Computer

In this exercise, you will disconnect all users from open files on your computer.

Note Only Partner B should complete this exercise; Partner A will be an observer.

▶ **To disconnect all users from open files on your computer**

1. In the console tree, under Shared Folders, make sure that Open Files is still selected.

2. On the Action menu, click Disconnect All Open Files.

   A Microsoft Management Console dialog box appears asking if you are sure you wish to close all resources.

3. Click OK.

   What happens?

---

4. Close all open windows, and log off.

Note The OpenTest file on Partner A's computer does not close on its own; he or she should close the file when the exercise is completed. If time allows, Partner A and Partner B should swap roles and repeat Exercises 2, 3, and 4.

Lab 29: Creating Shared Folders

Objectives

After completing this lab, you will be able to

- Use the Computer Management snap-in to create a shared folder on your local computer.

- Use the Computer Management snap-in to create a shared folder on a remote computer.

- Create a custom console containing the Computer Management snap-in that allows you to choose the remote computer on which you want to manage network resources.

Estimated time to complete this lab: 20 minutes

Note You will be working in pairs in this lab. One of you will be Partner A, and one of you will be Partner B. Not all the procedures will be completed by both partners.

Exercise 1
Creating a Shared Folder on Your Local Computer Using Computer Management

In this exercise, you will use the Computer Management snap-in to create a shared folder on your local computer.

Note Both partners should complete this exercise.

▶ **To create a new shared folder on your computer using Computer Management**

1. Log on to your local computer as Student*z* using a password of "password".
2. Open Windows Explorer, and then create two folders: C:\Library and C:\SciLib.
3. Click the Start button, point to Programs, point to Administrative Tools, and then click Computer Management.
4. In the console tree, under Shared Folders, click Shares.
5. On the Action menu, click New File Share.

   The Create Shared Folder wizard starts.
6. In the Folder To Share text box, type **C:\Library**.
7. Type **Library** in the Share Name text box, and then click Next.

   A final page of four basic share permission options appears.

   What permission is set by default?

8. Click the Finish button to accept the default permission.

   The Create Shared Folders dialog box appears telling you that the share has been successfully created and asking you whether or not you want to create another shared folder.
9. Click the No button.

Exercise 2
Creating a Shared Folder on a Remote Computer

In this exercise, you will create a custom MMC console containing the Computer Management snap-in and point it at your partner's computer. You will then use this custom MMC console to create a shared folder on your partner's computer.

Note Both partners should complete this exercise.

▶ **To create a shared folder on a remote computer**

1. On the Start menu, click Run, type **mmc**, and then click OK.

   A custom console appears.

2. On the Console menu, click Add/Remove Snap-In.

   The Add/Remove Snap-In dialog box appears.

3. Click the Add button.

   The Add Standalone Snap-In dialog box appears.

4. In the Add Standalone Snap-In dialog box, click Computer Management and then click the Add button.

   The Computer Management dialog box appears.

5. In the Computer Management dialog box, select the Another Computer radio button and then click the Browse button.

   The Select Computer dialog box appears.

6. In the Name text box, select Computer*p* (your partner's computer) and then click OK.

7. Select the Allow The Selected Computer To Be Changed When Launching From The Command Line. This Only Applies If You Save The Console check box.

8. Click the Finish button, and close the Add Standalone Snap-In dialog box.

9. Click OK to close the Add/Remove Snap-In dialog box.

10. On the Console menu, click Save.

    The Save As dialog box appears.

11. In the File Name text box, type **RSF** and then click the Save button.

Note RSF is an acronym for Remote Shared Folders.

12. In the console tree of the RSF console, expand Computer Management, expand Shared Folders, and click Shares.

13. On the Action menu, click New File Share.

    The Create Shared Folder wizard starts. Notice that it is pointing to Computer*p* (your partner's computer).

14. In the Folder To Share text box, type **C:\SciLib**, and in the Share Name text box, type **SciLib**.

15. In the Share Description text box, type **Science Library** and then click Next.

    A page of four basic share permission options appears.

16. Select the Customize Share And Folder Permissions radio button, and then click the Custom button.

    The Customize Permissions dialog box appears.

17. Change the permissions so that Everyone can read the articles in the Science Library, but they cannot change them.

18. Click the Add button.

    The Select Users, Computers, Or Groups dialog box appears.

19. Make sure that you select Corpy.Corp.Com in the Look In drop-down list in the Select Users, Computers, Or Groups dialog box, and then add the Administrators group.

20. Click OK.

    The Customize Permissions dialog box re-appears.

21. Allow Administrators to have Full Control, and then click OK.

22. Click the Finish button on the Create Shared Folder wizard.

    The Create Shared Folder dialog box appears, telling you that the share has been successfully created and asking you whether you want to create another shared folder.

23. Click the No button.

    Was the SciLib folder shared? How can you tell?

    _____

24. Close the Remote Shared Folders snap-in, and when prompted to Save Console Settings, click the Yes button.

25. Close all windows.

Exercise 3
Choosing the Remote Computer on Which to Manage Resources

In this exercise, you will use a custom MMC console containing the Computer Management snap-in that allows you to choose on which computer you want to create and manage shares.

Note Both partners should complete this exercise.

▶ **To launch a custom console from a command line**

1. On the Start menu, point to Programs, point to Accessories, and click Command Prompt.

   The Command Prompt window appears.

2. At the command prompt, type **cd c:\documents and settings\student**z**\start menu\programs\administrative tools** and press ENTER.

Note Replace the z in student$z$ with your student number.

It is difficult to type a long path correctly, so you may want to do a series of CD commands instead to reach the final folder.

3. Type **mmc rsf.msc**, and press ENTER.

4. In the console tree, select Computer Management (Computer$p$) (your partner's computer).

5. Click the Action menu.

   Notice that Connect To Another Computer is now an option on the Action menu. On the Action menu, click Connect To Another Computer.

   The Select Computer dialog box appears.

6. Select one of the listed computers from the Name list box, and then click OK.

Note You can choose your partner's computer or any other computer listed.

7. Close all windows and log off.

Lab 30: Sending Console Messages

Objectives

After completing this lab, you will be able to

- Send a console message.

Estimated time to complete this lab: 5 minutes

Exercise 1
Sending a Console Message

In this exercise, you will use the Shared Folders snap-in to send a console message.

Note Both partners should complete this exercise.

▶ **To send a console message**

1. Log on to your local computer as Administrator using a password of "password".

2. Click the Start button, point to Programs, point to Administrative Tools, and then click Computer Management.

3. In the console tree, click Shared Folders.

4. On the Action menu, point to All Tasks and then click Send Console Message.

   The Send Console Message dialog box appears.

5. In the Message text box, type **Computer1 is shutting down in 5 minutes.**

6. Click the Add button.

   The Add Recipients dialog box appears.

7. In the Recipients text box, type **Computer*p*** (where *p* is your partner's student number).

8. Click OK.

9. Click the Send button.

   A Send Console Message message box appears briefly on your computer showing that the message is being sent.

   A Messenger Service message box appears on your partner's computer, displaying the message you sent.

10. Your partner clicks OK to close the Messenger Service message box.

11. Close all open windows, and then log off.

Lab 31: Configuring an Inbound Connection

Objectives

After completing this lab, you will be able to

- Use the Network Connections wizard to configure an inbound connection.

Estimated time to complete this lab: 10 minutes

Exercise 1
Configuring an Inbound Connection

In this exercise, you will configure an inbound connection.

▶   **To configure an inbound connection**

1. Log on to your local computer as Administrator using a password of "password".

2. Click the Start button, point to Settings, and then click Network And Dial-Up Connections.

   The Network And Dial-Up Connections window appears.

   Scroll through the information listed in the left pane, and list the five tasks you can perform using this window.

   _____

   _____

   _____

3. Double-click the Make New Connection icon.

   The Welcome To The Network Connection Wizard page appears.

4. Click Next.

   The Network Connection Type page appears.

5. Review the available options on the Network Connection Type page.

6. Select the Accept Incoming Connections radio button, and then click Next.

   The Devices For Incoming Connections page appears.

7. Under Connection Devices, select the modem device check box for your computer.

Note If your computer does not have a modem installed, the Devices For Incoming Connections page will not appear.

8. If you have a modem installed on your computer, click the Properties button and select the Disconnect A Call If Idle For More Than ____ Minutes check box.

   What is the default setting for the number of minutes to be exceeded to disconnect an idle call?

   _____

9. Click OK to accept the default settings and return to the Devices For Incoming Connections page, and then click Next.

   The Incoming Virtual Private Connection page appears.

10. Under Choose Whether To Allow Virtual Private Connections, select the Allow Virtual Private Connections radio button and then click Next.

    The Allowed Users page appears.

11. Under Users Allowed To Connect, select the Administrator check box and then click the Properties button.

    The Administrator Properties dialog box appears.

12. Click the Callback tab.

13. Review the Callback tab's options, make sure the default Do Not Allow Callback radio button is selected, and then click OK.

    The Allowed Users page reappears.

14. Click Next.

    The Networking Components page appears.

15. Under Networking Components, review the networking components available to you, click Internet Protocol TCP/IP, and then click the Properties button.

    The Incoming TCP/IP Properties dialog box appears.

16. Select the Specify TCP/IP Addresses radio button.

17. In the From text box, type **10.1.1.1**, and in the To text box, type **10.1.1.99** and then click OK.

Note Your instructor will tell you if there is a valid address that you can use to test your inbound connection.

The Networking Components page reappears.

18. Click Next.

    The Completing The Network Connection Wizard page appears. You are prompted to enter a name for the connection.

19. Click the Finish button to accept the default Incoming Connections in The Connection Will Be Named text box.

    The Network And Dial-Up Connections window reappears. Notice that the Incoming Connections icon has been created and is now shown in the window.

    Leave the Network And Dial-Up Connections window open for the next lab.

Lab 32: Configuring an Outbound Connection

Objectives

After completing this lab, you will be able to

■ Use the Network Connections wizard to configure an outbound connection.

Estimated time to complete this lab: 10 minutes

Exercise 1
Configuring an Outbound Connection

In this exercise, you will configure an outbound connection.

▶   **To configure an outbound connection**

1. Ensure that you are logged on to your local computer as Administrator using a password of "password".

2. In the Network And Dial-Up Connections window, double-click the Make New Connection icon.

   The Welcome To The Network Connection Wizard page appears.

3. Click Next.

   The Network Connection Type page appears.

4. Select the Connect To A Private Network Through The Internet radio button, and then click Next.

5. If the Public Network page appears, select the Do Not Dial The Initial Connection radio button and then click Next.

   The Destination Address page appears.

6. In the Host Name Or IP Address (such as Microsoft.com or 123.45.6.78) text box, type **10.1.1.*a*** and then click Next.

Note Your instructor will tell you if there is a valid address that you can use to test your inbound connection. If there is no valid address, start a command prompt, run ipconfig, and then determine the IP address of your computer. Replace *a* with the last octet of your IP address. If you need help with running ipconfig, refer to Chapter 7 of the *ALS: Microsoft Windows 2000 Professional* textbook.

   The Connection Availability page appears.

7. Under Create This Connection, select the Only For Myself radio button and then click Next.

   The Completing The Network Connection Wizard page appears.

   You are prompted to enter a name for the connection.

   Notice at the bottom of the page there is a check box that will have a shortcut for this connection created on your desktop.

8. Click the Finish button to accept the default Virtual Private Connection in the Type The Name You Want To Use For This Connection text box.

   The Connect Virtual Private Connection dialog box appears.

9. Ensure that Administrator is entered into the User Name text box, and type **password** in the Password text box.

Note If your computer is on a network and you entered a valid address in step 6, enter a valid user name and password here.

10. Click the Connect button.

Note If you entered a valid address in step 6 and you entered a valid user name and password in step 9, a message will be displayed stating that the Virtual Private Connection is now connected. If you entered your own IP address, the operation will fail.

The Connecting Virtual Private Connection message box displays while your computer attempts to make the connection.

11. If your connection fails, click Cancel.

12. If you connect successfully to another computer, the Connection Complete message box appears.

13. Click OK.

14. Click the Virtual Private Connection icon in the system tray.

The Virtual Private Connection Status dialog box appears.

15. Click the Disconnect button.

16. Close all windows, and log off.

Lab 33: Installing and Using the Microsoft Windows 2000 Recovery Console

Objectives

After completing this lab, you will be able to

- View the files used during the Windows 2000 boot process.
- Install and use the Windows 2000 Recovery Console.
- Use Computer Management to start a service.

Estimated time to complete this lab: 15 minutes

Exercise 1
Viewing Files Used in the Windows 2000 Boot Process

In this exercise, you will view the files used in the Windows 2000 boot process.

▶   **To view files used in the boot process**

1. Log on to your local computer as Administrator using a password of "password".

2. Start Windows Explorer, and select Local Disk (C:).

   Windows Explorer starts and displays the folders and files located on local disk C.

   Which files are listed?

   _____

   _____

   _____

3. On the Tools menu, click Folder Options.

   The Folder Options dialog box appears.

4. Click the View tab.

5. On the View tab, clear the check box in front of Hide File Extensions For Known File Types.

6. Select the Show Hidden Files And Folders radio button, and then click OK.

   Which files are now listed?

   _____

7. On the Tools menu, click Folder Options.

8. On the View tab, clear the check box in front of Hide Protected Operating System Files (Recommended).

   A Warning message box appears, telling you that you have chosen to display protected operating system files (files labeled system and hidden) and asking you if you are sure you want to display them.

9. Click the Yes button to close the message box, and then click OK to close the Folder Options dialog box.

Notice that there are more files listed, including the following: Boot.ini, Ntdetect.com, and Ntldr. Please complete the following table:

File	Function
Boot.ini	_____
	_____
	_____
	_____
Ntldr	_____
	_____
	_____
	_____
Ntdetect.com	_____
	_____
	_____
	_____

10. Expand C:\Winnt\System32.

You are prompted to click the Show Files hyperlink to view the contents of this folder.

11. Click Show Files, and locate Ntoskrnl.exe and Hal.dll.

12. Close Windows Explorer, and log off.

Exercise 2
Installing the Windows 2000 Recovery Console

In this exercise, you will install the Recovery Console.

▶ **To install the Recovery Console**

1. Log on to the Corp*y* domain (where *y* is the number your instructor has assigned to your domain) as Student*z* (where *z* is your student number) using a password of "password".

2. Start Windows Explorer, and on the Tools menu, click Map Network Drive.

   The Map Network Drive dialog box appears.

3. In the Drive drop-down list, select W:.

4. In the Folder combo box, type **\\instructor*x*\w2000pro** and then click the Finish button.

Note Remember to replace the *x* in \\instructor*x* with the number of your instructor's computer.

   The W2000Pro On 'Instructor*x*' window appears.

5. Click the Start button, and then click Run.

   The Run dialog box appears.

6. In the Open combo box, type **w:\i386\winnt32 /cmdcon** and then click OK.

   The Windows 2000 Setup dialog box appears asking if you want to install the Recovery Console.

7. Click the Yes button.

   Windows 2000 Setup installs the Windows 2000 Recovery Console. Depending on the speed of the network and the number of students installing, this could take a couple of minutes.

8. When the installation has completed, the Microsoft Windows 2000 Professional Setup message box appears to inform you that the Windows 2000 Recovery Console has been successfully installed.

9. Click OK to close the message box.

Exercise 3
Using the Windows 2000 Recovery Console

In this exercise, you will use the Help command to view the available commands. You will then use the Listsvc command to view the available services and the Disable command to disable the Alerter service.

▶ **To use the Recovery Console**

1. Close all open windows, and restart your computer.

2. Select Microsoft Windows 2000 Recovery Console from the Bootstrap Loader menu.

   The Microsoft Windows 2000 Recovery Console starts and prompts you to select which Windows 2000 installation you would like to log on to.

   Note If you have more than one Windows installation on this computer, each installation will be listed here.

3. Type **1**, and then press ENTER.

   You are prompted to enter the Administrator password.

4. Type **password**, and then press ENTER.

5. At the command prompt, type **help** and then press ENTER.

6. Press the SPACEBAR to scroll through the list of available commands a page at a time.

   Notice the Disable command and the Listsvc command.

7. At the command prompt, type **listsvc** and press ENTER.

   Notice that the Listsvc command lists all available services and their Startup Type values for the current Windows 2000 installation. Notice that the Alerter service is listed and its Startup Type option is set to Manual.

8. Press the SPACEBAR to scroll through the list of services a page at a time.

9. Press ESC to stop.

10. At the command prompt, type **disable /?** and then press ENTER.

    Note The Disable command allows you to disable a Windows 2000 system service or driver.

11. At the command prompt, type **disable alerter** and then press ENTER.

   Recovery Console displays several lines of text describing how the registry entry for the Alerter service has been modified.

   According to the information on your screen, what was the Alerter service Startup Type value?

   _____

   According to the information on your screen, what is the new Startup Type value for the Alerter service?

   _____

   According to the information on your screen, when do the changes take effect?

   _____

12. At the command prompt, type **exit** and then press ENTER to restart your computer.

Exercise 4
Restarting the Alerter Service

In this exercise, you will confirm that the Alerter service is disabled and then you will restart it.

▶ **To restart the Alerter service**

1. Log on to your local computer as Administrator with a password of "password".

2. Click the Start button, point to Programs, point to Administrative Tools, and then click Computer Management.

3. In the console tree of the Computer Management window, expand Services And Applications and then click Services.

   In the Details pane, notice that the Alerter service is disabled.

4. Double-click Alerter.

5. The Alerter Properties (Local Computer) dialog box appears.

6. In the Startup Type drop-down list, change the Startup Type option to Automatic and then click OK.

7. In the Details pane of the Computer Management window, right-click Alerter and then click the Start button.

8. A Service Control message box appears while Alerter is starting.

   Notice that the Status for the Alerter service is now Started and the Startup Type option is Automatic.

9. Close the Computer Management window.

10. Close all windows, and log off.

Lab 34: Installing and Using the Microsoft Windows 2000 Installation Deployment Tools

Objectives

After completing this lab, you will be able to

- Extract the Windows 2000 installation deployment tools.
- Use Setup Manager to create an unattended setup script.

Estimated time to complete this lab: 40 minutes

Exercise 1
Extracting the Windows 2000 Installation Deployment Tools

In this exercise, you extract the Windows 2000 installation deployment tools from the Windows 2000 Professional installation files and copy them to your hard disk.

▶ **To install the Windows 2000 installation deployment tools**

1. Log on to the domain as Student$z$ (where z is your student number) using a password of "password".

2. Start Windows Explorer, and create a folder named Deploy in the root folder of drive C.

Note The Deploy folder will be used to contain the files extracted from the Deploy.cab file in the \\instructor$x$\w2000pro\Support\Tools shared folder containing the Windows 2000 Professional installation files.

3. Click the Start button, and then click Run.

   The Run dialog box appears.

4. In the Open text box, type **\\instructor$x$\w2000pro\support\tools** (where x is your instructor's computer number) and click OK.

   Windows Explorer appears, with the Tools folder active.

5. Double-click the Deploy file.

   The contents of the Deploy file appear in the Details pane.

6. On the Edit menu, click Select All.

Note You can also select all the files in the Deploy.cab file by holding down the CTRL key and then clicking each of the files listed. If your file icons are listed in one column, you can select the files by clicking the first file in the list, holding down the SHIFT key, and then clicking the last file in the list.

7. Right-click any of the selected files, and then click Extract on the menu that appears.

Note You can also extract the files in a .cab file, such as the Deploy.cab file, by clicking on the File menu and then clicking Extract.

The Browse For Folder dialog box appears.

8. Select the C:\Deploy folder, and then click OK.

   The Copying dialog box appears briefly as the files are extracted and copied to the Deploy folder on your computer.

9. In Windows Explorer, click the C:\Deploy folder in the console tree on your computer to view the contents.

   You should see the seven files from the Deploy file listed in the Details pane. These files have been extracted from the Deploy file and are now ready to use.

10. Double-click the Readme file.

11. Take a moment to view the topics covered in the Readme file, and then close Microsoft Notepad.

Exercise 2
Using the Setup Manager to Create an Unattended Setup Script

In this exercise, you will use the Windows 2000 Setup Manager to create an unattended setup script. At the same time, the Setup Manager wizard creates a distribution folder and a .UDP file.

▶   **To create an unattended setup script using the Setup Manager wizard**

1. In Windows Explorer, double-click the Setupmgr file.

   The Welcome To The Windows 2000 Setup Manager Wizard page appears.

2. Click Next.

   The New Or Existing Answer File page appears.

3. Ensure that the Create A New Answer File radio button is selected, and then click Next.

   The Product To Install page appears. Notice that you have three choices: Windows 2000 Unattended Installation, Sysprep Install, and Remote Installation Services.

4. Ensure that the Windows 2000 Unattended Installation radio button is selected, and then click Next.

   The Platform page appears. Notice you have two choices: Windows 2000 Professional and Windows 2000 Server.

5. Ensure that the Windows 2000 Professional radio button is selected, and then click Next.

   The User Interaction Level page appears. Notice that you have five choices:

   - **Provide Default**. The answers you provide in the answer file are the default answers that the user sees. The user may accept the default answers or change any of the answers supplied by the script.

   - **Fully Automated**. The installation is fully automated. The user does not have the chance to review or change the answers supplied by the script.

   - **Hide Pages**. The answers provided by the script are supplied during the installation. Any page for which the script supplies all answers is hidden from the user so that the user cannot review or change the answers supplied by the script.

   - **Read Only**. The script provides the answers, and the user may view the answers on any page that is not hidden, but the user may not change the answers.

   - **GUI Attended**. The text-mode portion of the installation is automated, but the user must supply the answers for the GUI-mode portion of the installation.

6. Select the Fully Automated radio button, and then click Next.

   The License Agreement page appears.

Note If you had chosen any option other than Fully Automated, the License Agreement page would not have been displayed.

---

7. Read the License Agreement, click the I Accept The Terms Of The License Agreement check box, and then click Next.

   The Customize The Software page appears.

8. Enter your name in the Name text box, enter your organization in the Organization text box, and then click Next.

   The Computer Names page appears. Notice that you have three choices:

   - You can enter a series of computer names to be used during the various iterations of the script in the Computer Name text box.

   - You can provide the name of a text file to import that has one computer name per line listed by clicking the Import button and then selecting the text file. Setup imports and uses these names as the computer names in the various iterations of the script.

   - You can select the Automatically Generate Computer Names Based On Organization Name check box to allow the system to automatically generate the computer names to be used.

9. Type **Computer$z$A** (where z is your student number) in the Computer Name text box, and then click the Add button. Repeat this step to add Computer$z$B and Computer$z$C to the list of computer names.

   Notice that the names Computer$z$A, Computer$z$B, and Computer$z$C appear under Computers To Be Installed.

10. Click Next.

    The Administrator Password page appears. Notice that you have two choices: Prompt The User For An Administrator Password and Use The Following Administrator Password (127 Characters Maximum).

Note On the User Interaction Level page, you selected Fully Automated, so the Prompt The User For An Administrator Password option is grayed out.

Notice that you can also have the administrator log on automatically, and you can set the number of times you want the administrator to log on automatically when the computer is restarted.

11. Ensure that the Use The Following Administrator Password (127 Characters Maximum) radio button is selected, type **password** in the Password and the Confirm Password text boxes, and then click Next.

The Display Settings page appears. Notice that you can set the Colors, Screen Area, and Refresh Frequency settings for the display. You can also choose Custom to create your own settings rather than pick from the selections listed under each of the three fields.

12. Click Next to accept the default settings.

The Network Settings page appears. Notice that you can choose Typical Settings—which installs TCP/IP, enables DHCP, and installs the Client for Microsoft Networks protocol for each destination computer—or you can choose Custom Settings.

13. Select the Custom Settings radio button, and then click Next.

The Number Of Network Adapters page appears.

14. Ensure that the default radio button, One Network Adapter, is selected, and then click Next.

Note Your instructor can tell you if there is more than one network adapter card in your computer.

The Networking Components page appears. Notice that the Client For Microsoft Networks, File And Printer Sharing For Microsoft Networks, and Internet Protocol (TCP/IP) components are installed by default.

15. Select Internet Protocol (TCP/IP), and then click the Properties button.

The Internet Protocol (TCP/IP) Properties dialog box appears, with the General tab active. Notice that the Obtain An IP Address Automatically radio button is selected by default and that this dialog box is identical to the one used to configure TCP/IP through Network Neighborhood.

16. Click Cancel, and then click Next to accept the default settings for networking components.

The Workgroup Or Domain page appears. Notice that the default option is Workgroup and the default workgroup name is Workgroup.

17. Select the Windows Server Domain radio button, and type **Corpy** (where y is the number your instructor has assigned to the domain) in the Windows Server Domain text box.

Notice that the Create A Computer Account In The Domain check box is not selected.

18. Select the Create A Computer Account In The Domain check box.

Notice that you can now specify a user account and password to use to create a computer account in the domain during installation.

19. In the User Name text box, type **Studentz** (where z is your student number), in the Password and Confirm Password text boxes, type **password**, and then click Next.

The Time Zone page appears.

20. In the Time Zone drop-down list, select the appropriate time zone and then click Next.

    The Additional Settings page appears.

21. Ensure that the default radio button, Yes, Edit The Additional Settings, is selected, and then click Next.

    The Telephony page appears.

22. Select the appropriate setting from the What Country/Region Are You In? drop-down list.

23. Type the appropriate numbers in the What Area (Or City) Code Are You In? text box.

24. Type the appropriate number(s) in the If You Dial A Number To Access An Outside Line, What Is It? text box.

25. Select the appropriate setting from the The Phone System At This Location Uses: drop-down list, and then click Next.

    The Regional Settings page appears. The default selection is the Use The Default Regional Settings For The Windows Version You Are Installing radio button.

26. Click Next to accept the default.

    The Languages page appears. This page allows you to add support for additional languages.

27. Click Next to accept the default.

    The Browser And Shell Settings page appears. Notice that you can choose from the following three settings: Use Default Internet Explorer Settings, Use An Autoconfiguration Script Created By The Internet Explorer Administration Kit To Configure Your Browser, and Individually Specify Proxy And Default Home Page Settings.

28. Click Next to accept the default radio button, Use Default Internet Explorer Settings.

    The Installation Folder page appears. Notice that you can select from three options: A Folder Named Winnt, A Uniquely Named Folder Generated By Setup, and This Folder.

29. Select the This Folder radio button, in the This Folder text box, type **w2000pro**, and then click Next.

    The Install Printers page appears.

30. Click Next to continue without having the script install any network printers.

    The Run Once page appears. This page allows you to configure Windows 2000 Professional to run one or more commands the first time a user logs on.

31. Click Next to continue without having the script run any additional commands.

    The Distribution Folder page appears. This page allows you to have the Setup Manager wizard create a distribution folder on your computer or network with the required Windows 2000 installation files. You can add additional files to this distribution folder.

    Note For instance, if you were upgrading systems to Windows 2000 Professional, you could add any application update packs to the distribution folder and enter the commands to apply the update packs to the application as part of the upgrade.

32. Ensure that the default radio button, Yes, Create Or Modify A Distribution Folder, is selected, and then click Next.

    Note The other option is No, This Answer File Will Be Used To Install From A CD. If you are going to be doing a large number of installations, you do not want to do simultaneous installations to multiple computers from a CD-ROM. Instead, create one or more distribution folders.

    The Distribution Folder Name page appears. Notice that the default distribution folder name is C:\win2000dist and is shared as win2000dist.

33. Ensure that the default radio button, Create A New Distribution Folder, is selected, and then click Next.

    The Additional Mass Storage Drivers page appears. Notice that this page allows you to add new or additional mass storage drivers during installation.

34. Click Next to continue without adding any additional drivers.

    The Hardware Abstraction Layer (HAL) page appears. This page allows you to replace the default HAL.

35. Click Next to use the default HAL.

    The Additional Commands page appears. This page allows you to specify additional commands to be run at the end of the unattended Setup.

36. Click Next to continue without running any additional commands.

    The OEM Branding page appears. This page allows you to customize Windows 2000 Professional Setup by adding your company's original equipment manufacturer's (OEM) branding. You may specify both a logo bitmap and a background bitmap.

37. Click Next to continue without specifying any OEM branding.

    The Additional Files Or Folders page appears. This page allows you to specify additional files or folders to be copied to the destination computers.

38. Click Next to continue without specifying any additional files or folders to copy.

   The Answer File Name page appears.

39. Click Next to continue and accept the default Location And File Name of C:\Win2000dist\unattend.txt.

   The Location Of Setup Files page appears. The files can be copied from the CD-ROM, or you can specify a network location.

40. Select the Copy The Files From This Location radio button, type **\\instructor:x\w2000pro\i386** (where *x* is your instructor's computer number), and click Next.

   The Copying Files page appears while the Setup Manager wizard copies the distribution files. This will take a few minutes. An indicator bar shows you the progress of the copy operation.

   The Completing The Windows 2000 Setup Manager Wizard page appears.

   Notice that Setup created and shared a C:\Win2000dist folder. Notice also that Setup created three new files in C:\Win2000dist: Unattend.txt, Unattend.udf, and Unattend.bat.

41. Click the Finish button.

▶   **To verify the existence of the distribution files**

1. In Windows Explorer, double-click the C:\Win2000dist folder to view the distribution files.

2. Close Windows Explorer.

3. Log off your computer.

Lab 35: Using the System Preparation Tool

Objectives

After completing this lab, you will be able to

- Use the System Preparation tool to create a master disk image.

- Use the System Preparation tool to install Microsoft Windows 2000 Professional.

- Use the Setup Manager to create an Answer file for an unattended Sysprep Installation.

- Use the System Preparation tool with an Answer file to install Windows 2000 Professional.

Note If you completed Exercise 1 of Lab 34, you can skip to Exercise 2 of this lab.

Estimated time to complete this lab: 40 minutes

Exercise 1
Extracting the Windows 2000 Deployment Tools

In this exercise, you extract the Windows 2000 installation deployment tools from the Windows 2000 Professional installation files and copy them to your hard disk.

▶ **To install the Windows 2000 Deployment Tools**

1. Log on to the domain as Student*z* (where *z* is your student number) using a password of "password".

2. Start Windows Explorer, and create a folder named Deploy in the root folder of drive C.

Note The Deploy folder will be used to contain the files extracted from the Deploy.cab file in the shared folder containing the Windows 2000 Professional installation files.

---

3. Click the Start button, and then click Run.

   The Run dialog box appears.

4. In the Open text box, type **\\instructor*x*\w2000pro\support\tools** (where *x* is your instructor's computer number) and click OK.

5. Double-click the Deploy file.

   Windows Explorer appears, with the Tools folder active.

   The contents of the Deploy file appear in the Details pane.

6. On the Edit menu, click Select All.

Note You can also select all the files in the Deploy.cab file by holding down the CTRL key and then clicking each of the files listed. If your file icons are listed in one column, you can select the files by clicking the first file in the list, holding down the SHIFT key, and then clicking the last file in the list.

---

7. Right-click any of the selected files, and then click Extract on the menu that appears.

Note You can also extract the files in the Deploy.cab file by clicking on the File menu and then clicking Extract.

The Browse For Folder dialog box appears.

8. Select the C:\Deploy folder, and then click OK.

   The Copying dialog box appears briefly as the files are extracted and copied to the Deploy folder on your computer.

9. In Windows Explorer, click the C:\Deploy folder on your computer to view the contents.

   You should see the seven files from the Deploy file listed in the Details pane. These files have been extracted from the Deploy file and are now ready to use.

10. Double-click the Readme file.

11. Take a moment to view the topics covered in the Readmefile, and then close Notepad.

Exercise 2
Using the System Preparation Tool to Create a Master Disk Image

In this exercise, you will use the Windows 2000 System Preparation tool to create a master disk image.

Caution If you complete the following exercise, you will have to reinstall Windows 2000 Professional on your computer.

▶ **To create a master disk image**

1. If you skipped Exercise 1 of this lab, log on to the domain as Student*z* (where *z* is your student number) using a password of "password".

2. In Windows Explorer, double-click the Sysprep file in the C:\Deploy folder.

   A Windows 2000 System Preparation Tool message box appears, warning you that running Sysprep might modify some of the security parameters of the system.

Note If you run Sysprep.exe on your computer, you will lose some of the computer's security parameters.

3. If you are certain that you don't mind having to reinstall Windows 2000 Professional, click OK to continue.

4. Your computer shuts down and prompts you to turn it off.

5. Turn your computer off.

Note You can run the Setup Manager wizard to create a Sysprep.inf file. Sysprep.inf provides answers to the Windows 2000 Professional Setup wizard on the destination computers. You can also use this file to specify customized drivers. The Setup Manager wizard creates a Sysprep folder at the root of the drive image and places Sysprep.inf in this folder. The Windows 2000 Professional Setup wizard checks for Sysprep.inf in the Sysprep folder at the root of the drive on which Windows 2000 Professional is being installed.

Exercise 3
Using the System Preparation Tool to Install Windows 2000 Professional

In this exercise, you use a master disk image to install Windows 2000 Professional. In Exercise 2, you created a master disk image. Normally you would use a third-party tool to copy the disk image to another computer and preserve the master disk image. For the purposes of this exercise, you will reinstall Windows 2000 Professional using your computer and the master disk image you created on it.

▶ **To install Windows 2000 Professional using a master disk image**

1. Power on your computer.

   After a few minutes, the Windows 2000 Professional Setup wizard appears, displaying the License Agreement page.

2. Read through the license agreement, click the I Accept This Agreement check box, and then click Next.

   The Regional Settings page appears.

3. Ensure that the System Locale, the User Locale, and the Keyboard Layout options are correct, and then click Next.

   The Personalize Your Software page appears.

4. In the Name text box, type your name; in the Organization text box, type your organization; and then click Next.

   The Your Product Key page appears.

5. Enter your product key, and then click Next.

   Note Your instructor will provide you with the product key.

   The Computer Name And Administrator Password page appears.

6. In the Computer Name text box, type **Computer$z$** (where z is your student number).

7. In the Password and Confirm Password text boxes, type **password**, and then click Next.

   Note If a modem is connected to the computer on which you are installing Windows 2000 Professional, Setup displays the Modem Dialing Information dialog box; otherwise, Setup displays the Date And Time Settings page. If your computer doesn't have a modem, go to step 12.

   The Modem Dialing Information page appears.

8. Select the appropriate setting from the What Country/Region Are You In? drop-down list.

9. Type the appropriate numbers in the What Area Or City Code Are You In? text box.

10. Type the appropriate number(s) in the If You Dial A Number To Access An Outside Line, What Is It? text box.

11. Select the appropriate setting from the The Phone System At This Location Uses: drop-down list, and then click Next.

   The Date And Time Settings page appears.

12. Ensure that the Date, Time, Time Zone, and the setting for Daylight Savings Time are correct, and then click Next. This takes a few minutes.

   The Networking Settings page appears.

13. Ensure that the Typical Settings radio button is selected, and then click Next.

   The Workgroup Or Computer Domain page appears.

14. Select the Yes, Make This Computer A Member Of The Following Domain radio button, in the Workgroup Or Computer Domain text box, type **Corp**y (where y is the number assigned to the domain by your instructor), and then click Next.

   The Join Computer To Corp$y$ Domain dialog box appears.

15. In the User Name text box, type **Student**z (where z is your student number), in the Password text box, type **password**, and then click OK.

   The Completing The Windows 2000 Setup Wizard page appears.

16. Click the Finish button.

   Your computer restarts, and then the Welcome To The Network Identification Wizard page appears.

17. Click Next.

   The User Account page appears. This page allows you to add a user account to the local security database on the computer. The account you add must exist in the Corp$y$ security database.

18. Ensure that the Add The Following User radio button is selected.

19. In the User Name text box, type **User77**.

20. In the User Domain text box, type **Corp**y, and then click Next.

   The Access Level page appears. Notice that you have three options:

   - **Standard User (Power Users Group)**. Selecting this radio button enables the user that you create, User77, to modify the computer and install programs but does not permit the user you create to read files that belong to other users.

   - **Restricted User (Users Group)**. Selecting this radio button enables the user that you create, User 77, to operate the computer and save documents, but does not permit the user you create to install programs or make potentially damaging changes to the system files and settings.

- **Other**. Selecting this radio button activates a pull-down menu that allows you to choose a group from all the groups on the computer, including the Administrators group.

21. Ensure that the Standard User (Power Users Group) radio button is selected, and then click Next.

What happens? Why?

_____

_____

_____

_____

22. Click OK to close the Access Level message box.

23. Click the Back button.

The User Account page appears.

24. Select the Do Not Add A User At This Time radio button, and then click Next.

The Completing The Network Identification Wizard page appears.

25. Click the Finish button.

26. Log on to the Corp*y* domain as Student*z* with a password of "password".

27. Click the Start button, point to Programs, point to Administrative Tools, and then click Computer Management.

28. In the console pane, expand Local Users And Groups.

29. Expand Groups, and then expand Users.

Are there groups listed other than the standard groups that are normally created during a Windows 2000 Professional installation? Are there additional users created? Why?

_____

_____

_____

_____

_____

_____

Exercise 4
Using the Setup Manager to Create an Answer File for Sysprep Installation

In this exercise, you will use the Windows 2000 Setup Manager to create an Answer file for Sysprep.

▶ **To create an unattended setup script using the Setup Manager wizard**

1. In Windows Explorer, open the C:\Deploy folder and then double-click the Setupmgr file.

   The Welcome To The Windows 2000 Setup Manager Wizard page appears.

2. Click Next.

   The New Or Existing Answer File page appears.

3. Ensure that the Create A New Answer File radio button is selected, and then click Next.

   The Product To Install page appears. Notice that you have three choices: Windows 2000 Unattended Installation, Sysprep Install, and Remote Installation Services.

4. Select the Sysprep Install radio button, and then click Next.

   The Platform page appears. Notice you have two choices: Windows 2000 Professional or Windows 2000 Server.

5. Ensure that the Windows 2000 Professional radio button is selected, and then click Next.

   The License Agreement page appears.

6. Read the License Agreement page.

   Notice that you have two choices: Yes, Fully Automate The Installation and No, Do Not Fully Automate The Installation. Notice that if you choose No, the end user must accept the End User License Agreement (EULA).

7. Select the Yes, Fully Automate The Installation radio button, and then click Next.

   The Customize The Software page appears.

8. Enter your name in the Name text box, enter your organization in the Organization text box, and then click Next.

   The Computer Name page appears.

9. Type **Computer***z* (where *z* is your student number) in the Computer Name text box, and then click Next.

   The Administrator Password page appears. Notice that you have two choices: Prompt The User For An Administrator Password and Use The Following Administrator Password (127 Characters Maximum).

Note The Prompt The User For An Administrator Password option is grayed out.

Notice that you can also have the administrator log on automatically, and you can set the number of times you want the administrator to log on automatically when the computer is restarted.

10. Type **password** in the Password and the Confirm Password text boxes, and then click Next.

   The Display Settings page appears. Notice that you can set the Colors, Screen Area, and Refresh Frequency settings for the display. You can also choose Custom to create your own settings rather than pick from the selections listed under each of the three fields.

11. Click Next to accept the default settings.

   The Network Settings page appears. Notice that you can choose Typical Settings—which installs TCP/IP, enables DHCP, and installs the Client for Microsoft Networks protocol for each destination computer—or you can choose Custom Settings.

12. Ensure that the Typical Settings radio button is selected, and then click Next.

   The Workgroup Or Domain page appears. Notice that the default option is Workgroup and the default workgroup name is Workgroup.

13. Click the Windows Server Domain radio button, and then type **Corpy** in the Windows Server Domain text box.

   Notice that the Create A Computer Account In The Domain check box is not selected.

14. Select the Create A Computer Account In The Domain check box.

   Notice that you can now specify a user account and password to use to create a computer account in the domain during installation.

15. In the User Name text box, type **Student**z (where z is your student number), and in the Password and Confirm Password text boxes, type **password**, and then click Next.

   The Time Zone page appears.

16. In the Time Zone drop-down list, select the appropriate time zone and then click Next.

   The Additional Settings page appears.

17. Ensure that the default radio button, Yes, Edit The Additional Settings, is selected, and then click Next.

   The Telephony page appears.

18. Select the appropriate setting from the What Country/Region Are You In? drop-down list.

19. Type the appropriate numbers in the What Area (Or City) Code Are You In? text box.

20. Type the appropriate number(s) in the If You Dial A Number To Access An Outside Line, What Is It? text box.

21. Select the appropriate setting from the The Phone System At This Location Uses: drop-down list, and then click Next.

    The Regional Settings page appears. The default selection is the Use The Default Regional Settings For The Windows Version You Are Installing radio button.

22. Click Next to accept the default.

    The Languages page appears. This page allows you to add support for additional languages.

23. Click Next to accept the default option.

    The Install Printers page appears.

24. Click Next to continue without having the script install any network printers.

    The Run Once page appears. This page allows you to configure Windows 2000 Professional to run one or more commands the first time a user logs on.

25. Click Next to continue without having the script run any additional commands.

    The Sysprep Folder page appears. If you are going to run Sysprep on this computer, the Setup Manager wizard can create a Sysprep folder that contains the files you need to run Sysprep and to customize your Sysprep installation.

Note The Sysprep folder will be removed by the system after Sysprep has finished.

26. Ensure that the default radio button, Yes, Create Or Modify The Sysprep Folder, is selected, and then click Next.

    The Additional Commands page appears. This page allows you to specify additional commands to be run at the end of the unattended Setup.

27. Click Next to continue without running any additional commands.

    The OEM Branding page appears. This page allows you to customize Windows 2000 Professional Setup by adding your company's OEM branding. You may specify both a logo bitmap and a background bitmap.

28. Click Next to continue without specifying any OEM branding.

    The Additional Files Or Folders page appears. This page allows you to specify additional files or folders to be copied to the destination computers.

29. Click Next to continue without specifying any additional files or folders to copy.

    A Windows 2000 Setup Manager Wizard message box appears, indicating that you must specify the location of certain files, such as Sysprep.exe.

30. Click OK.

    These files are located in the C:\Deploy folder. The Open dialog box appears, prompting you to confirm the location of the requested files.

31. Click the Open button.

    If a second dialog box appears requesting the location of a file, follow the same procedure—click OK to clear the error box and Open to confirm the location of the file.

    An OEM Duplicator String page appears.

32. In the Sysprep Information text box, type **Sysprep image created on** *mm*/*dd*/ *yyyy*.

Note Replace *mm* with the month, *dd* with the day and *yyyy* with the year. For example, if the Sysprep image is created on November 11, 2000, you would type 11/11/2000.

---

33. Click Next.

    The Answer File Name page appears. Notice that the default location and file name is C:\Deploy\Sysprep.inf.

Note If that is not the location you would like to use, you can change the path.

---

34. Click Next to accept the default location of C:\Deploy\Sysprep.inf.

    The Completing The Windows 2000 Setup Manager Wizard page appears.

    Notice that Setup created two new files (Sysprep.inf and Sysprep.bat) in C:\Deploy.

35. Click the Finish button.

Exercise 5
Using the System Preparation Tool to Create a Master Disk Image Containing an Answer File for Sysprep

In this exercise, you use the Windows 2000 System Preparation tool to create a master disk image.

▶ **To create a master disk image**

1. In Windows Explorer, double-click the Sysprep.bat file in the C:\Deploy folder.

   A Windows 2000 System Preparation Tool message box appears, warning you that running Sysprep might modify some of the security parameters of the system.

Note If you run Sysprep on your computer, you will lose some of your computer's security parameters.

---

2. If you are certain that you don't mind having to reinstall Windows 2000 Professional, click OK to continue.

3. Your computer shuts down and prompts you to turn it off.

4. Turn your computer off.

Note You can run the Setup Manager wizard to create a Sysprep.inf file. Sysprep.inf provides answers to the Setup wizard on the destination computers. You can also use this file to specify customized drivers. The Setup Manager wizard creates a Sysprep folder at the root of the drive image and places Sysprep.inf in this folder. The Setup wizard checks for Sysprep.inf in the Sysprep folder at the root of the drive in which Windows 2000 Professional is being installed.

Exercise 6
Using the System Preparation Tool to Install Windows 2000 Professional

In this exercise, you use a master disk image containing an answer file, Sysprep.inf, and a Sysprep.bat file to install Windows 2000 Professional. This is the master disk image you created in Exercise 5.

▶ **To install Windows 2000 Professional using a master disk image**

1. Power on your computer.

   After a few minutes, the Product Key Page appears.

2. Enter your product key, and then click Next.

Note Your instructor can tell you what your product key is.

   The Windows 2000 Professional Setup wizard starts and automatically completes the Windows 2000 Professional installation.

   The Completing The Windows 2000 Setup Wizard page appears.

3. Click the Finish button.

4. Restart your computer.

5. Log on locally as Administrator with a password of "password" to confirm that the installation completed successfully.

6. Log off your computer.

Lab 36: Configuring Offline Folders and Files

Objectives

After completing this lab, you will be able to

- Configure a computer to use offline folders and files.
- Configure a share so other users can use the files offline.
- Configure Synchronization Manager.

Estimated time to complete this lab: 45 minutes

Note In this lab, you will be working in pairs.

Exercise 1
Configuring Offline Folders

In this exercise, you will configure your computer as if it were a laptop running Microsoft Windows 2000 Professional, so that you can work offline using offline folders and files.

Note Partner A and Partner B should both complete Exercise 1.

▶ **To configure offline folders and files**

1. Log on to the Corp*y* domain (where *y* is the number your instructor has assigned to your domain) as Student*z* (where *z* is your student number) using a password of "password".

2. Start Windows Explorer, and on the Tools menu, click Folder Options.

   The Folder Options dialog box appears.

3. Click the Offline Files tab.

4. Ensure that the Enable Offline Files and the Synchronize All Offline Files Before Logging Off check boxes are selected.

Note By default, the Enable Offline Files check box, the Synchronize All Offline Files Before Logging Off check box, and the Enable Reminders check box are selected in Windows 2000 Professional. Notice also that the reminder balloon is scheduled to display every 60 minutes.

5. Select the Place Shortcut To Offline Files Folder On The Desktop check box, and then click OK.

6. Minimize Windows Explorer.

   Notice the Shortcut To Offline Files icon now appears on your desktop.

Exercise 2
Enabling a Share to Provide Offline Folders

In this exercise, you will create a folder and share it. You will then configure the network share so that other users can access the files in the share and use them offline. Finally, you will create a text document in the Offline shared folder (to be used in the next exercise to test how offline folders and files work).

Note Partner A and Partner B should both complete Exercise 2.

▶ **To enable a network share to provide files to be used offline**

1. Maximize Windows Explorer.

2. Create a folder in the root folder of drive C:, and name it Offline.

3. Right-click the Offline folder, and then click Sharing.

   The Offline Properties dialog box appears with the Sharing tab active.

4. Select the Share This Folder radio button, and notice that by default the name of the share is Offline.

5. Click the Caching button.

   The Caching Settings dialog box appears.

6. Click the Setting drop-down list.

   Notice that Caching has the following three settings:

   ▪ **Manual Caching For Documents.** This is the default setting. Users must manually specify any documents that they want available when they are working offline. To ensure proper file sharing, the server version of the file is always opened.

   ▪ **Automatic Caching For Documents.** Opened files are automatically downloaded and made available when working offline. Older copies are automatically deleted to make way for newer and more recently accessed files. To ensure proper file sharing, the server version of the file is always opened.

Note If you select Automatic Caching For Documents, the automatically cached documents are marked as Temporarily Available Offline in the Offline folder. Since these files can be removed from the cache if the cache gets full, an automatically cached file may not be available when you are working offline.

   ▪ **Automatic Caching For Programs.** This setting is recommended for folders with read-only data or run-from-the-network applications. File sharing is not ensured. Opened files are automatically downloaded and made available when working offline. Older copies are automatically deleted to make room for newer and more recently accessed files.

7. Select the Automatic Caching For Documents option, and then click OK.

8. Click OK to close the Offline Properties dialog box.

9. Leave Windows Explorer open.

▶ **To create a text document**

1. Create a text document in the Offline folder, and name it Student$z$ (where z is your student number).

2. Open the Student$z$ text file, and type the following text: **This is a text document created by Student$z$ on Computer$z$.**

Note Replace the z in Student$z$ and in Computer$z$ with your student number.

3. Save and close the Student$z$ text document.

Exercise 3
Configuring Synchronization Manager

In this exercise, you will configure Synchronization Manager to synchronize files every time the user logs on or off.

Note Both partners should complete Exercise 3.

▶ **To configure Synchronization Manager**

1. Click the Start button, and then click Run.

   The Run dialog box appears.

2. In the Open combo box, type **\\Computer*p*** and then click OK.

Note Replace the *p* in Computer*p* with your partner's student number. For example, if your partner's student number is 12, you would type **Computer12**.

   The Computer*p* window appears.

3. Double-click the Offline icon.

   The Offline On Computer*p* window appears.

4. Double-click the text file created by your partner.

5. The Student*p* – Notepad window (where *p* is your partner's student number) appears.

6. Close Microsoft Notepad, and minimize Offline On Computer*p* window.

Note Windows Explorer for your computer should still be open from the last exercise.

7. On your computer's Windows Explorer, click the Tools menu and then click Synchronize.

   The Items To Synchronize dialog box appears.

8. Click \\Computer*p*\Offline On Computer*p*, and then click the Setup button.

   The Synchronization Settings dialog box appears, with the Logon/Logoff tab active.

9. Review the options on the Logon/Logoff tab, and then review the options on the On Idle tab and on the Scheduled tab.

10. On the Logon/Logoff tab under Automatically Synchronize The Selected Items, ensure that the check boxes for When I Log On To My Computer and When I Log Off My Computer are both selected.

11. Click OK, and then close the Items To Synchronize window.

Exercise 4
Testing Synchronization

In this exercise, Partner A will open a text document on Partner B's computer and make a change. Then Partner A will disconnect from the network to work offline. Partner A will make a change to the offline version of the file and then reconnect to the network to see how synchronization works.

Important Most of Exercise 4 will be done by Partner A only. There are a few steps (clearly marked) that will be done by Partner B.

▶ **To test offline folders and files**

1. Maximize the Offline On Computer*p* window, and then double-click the text file previously created by your partner.

   The Student*p* – Notepad window (where *p* is your partner's student number) appears.

2. Type the following text (where *z* is your student number): **Student*z* is making this modification.**

3. On the File menu, click Save.

Note Partner B performs step 4.

---

4. Open the Student*z* text file (where *z* is your student number) on your computer.

   Is the modification made by Partner A in your file? Why or why not?

   _____

   _____

   _____

   _____

Note Partner A performs steps 5, 6, and 7.

---

5. Unplug the network cable from the back of your computer.

   Notice that a balloon message appears, notifying you that the network cable is now unplugged.

6. In the Student*p* – Notepad window (where *p* is your partner's student number), type the following text (where *z* is your student number): **This is a second modification made by Student*z*.**

7. On the File menu, click Save.

Note Partner B performs step 8.

8. Exit Notepad, and then reopen your Student*z* text file window (where *z* is your student number).

   Is the second modification made by Partner A in your file? Why or why not?

   _____

   _____

   _____

Note Partner A performs steps 9 through 14.

9. Exit Notepad, and close all open windows.

10. Double-click Shortcut To Offline Files on your desktop.

    The Offline Files Folder window appears.

11. Double-click the Student*p* text file (where *p* is your partner's student number) in the Offline Files Folder window.

    The Student*p* (where *p* is your partner's student number) – Notepad window appears.

    You are now working offline on the cached version of your partner's text file stored on your hard disk.

12. Reconnect the network cable to your computer.

13. Type the following text (where *z* is your student number): **Student*z* is making a third change.**

14. On the File menu, click Save.

Note Partner B performs step 15.

15. Exit Notepad, and then reopen your Student*z* text file.

    Is the third modification made by Partner A in your file? Why or why not?

    _____

    _____

    _____

Note Partner A performs steps 16 and 17.

16. Exit Notepad, and close the Offline Files Folder window.

17. Log off your computer.

What happens?

_____

_____

_____

_____

Note Partner B performs steps 18 through 20.

18. Exit Notepad, and then reopen your Student*z* text file. Verify that the file was updated.

19. Exit Notepad.

20. Log off your computer.

Exercise 5
Testing Offline Folders and Files

In this exercise, Partner B will open a text document on Partner A's computer, then disconnect from the network so that Partner B can work offline. Partner B will make a change to the offline version of the file. Partner A will also make a change to the version of the same text file on her or his computer. Then Partner B will reconnect to the network to see how synchronization works.

Important Most of Exercise 4 will be done by Partner B only. There are a few steps (clearly marked) that will be done by Partner A.

▶ **To test offline folders and files**

1. Log on to the domain as Student$z$ (where z is your student number) using a password of "password".

2. Click the Start button, and then click Run.

3. In the Open box, type **\\Computer$p$**.

Note Replace the p in Computer$p$ with your partner's student number. For example, if your partner's student number is 11, you would type **Computer11**.

The Computer$p$ window appears.

4. Double-click the Offline share, and then double-click the text file previously created by your partner.

5. Type the following text (where z is your student number): **Student$z$ is making this modification.**

6. On the File menu, click Save.

Note Partner A performs step 7.

7. Use Windows Explorer to open the Student$z$ text file (where z is your student number) on your computer.

Is the modification made by Partner B in your file? Why or why not?

_____

_____

_____

Note Partner B performs steps 8, 9, and 10.

8. Unplug the network cable from the back of your computer.

   Notice that a balloon message appears, notifying you that the network cable is now unplugged.

9. Type the following text (where z is your student number): **This is a second modification made by Student$z$.**

10. On the File menu, click Save.

Note Partner A performs steps 11 and 12.

11. Type the following text: **How does synchronization work when both copies of the file change?**

12. On the File menu, click Save and then exit Notepad.

Note Partner B performs steps 13 through 20.

13. Exit Notepad, and close all open windows.

14. Double-click Shortcut To Offline Files on your desktop.

   The Offline Files Folder window appears.

15. Double-click the Student$p$ text file (where p is your partner's student number) in the Offline Files Folder window.

   You are now working offline on the cached version of your partner's text file stored on your hard disk.

16. Reconnect the network cable to your computer.

17. Type the following text (where z is your student number): **Student$z$ is making a third change.**

18. On the File menu, click Save.

19. Close all open windows, and then log off.

   What happens?

   _____

   _____

   _____

20. Ensure that the Keep Both Versions. Save The Version On My Computer To The Network As: Student$z$ (student$z$ v1).txt radio button is selected, and click OK to close the dialog box.

   A Synchronization Complete message box appears briefly.

Note The Synchronization Complete message box may display an error message to inform you that an error occurred while synchronizing your data. If so, close the message box to continue. If you received an error during synchronization when you logged off, the Resolve File Conflicts dialog box reappears, indicating that both versions of the file changed and asking how you would like to resolve the conflict. Ensure that the default to keep both versions is selected. Click OK to close the dialog box.

In the Offline Files Folder window on Partner A's computer, how many files are there? What files are listed? Why?

_____

_____

_____

_____

_____

Note Both partners perform step 21.

21. Log off your computer.

Lab 37: Configuring Power Options

Objectives

After completing this lab, you will be able to

- Configure Power options.

Estimated time to complete this lab: 5 minutes

Exercise 1
Configuring Power Options

In this exercise, you will use Control Panel to configure Power options.

▶   **To configure Power options**

1. Log on to the domain as Student$z$ (where z is your student number) using a password of "password".

2. Start Control Panel, and then double-click Power Options.

    The Power Options Properties dialog box appears, with the Power Schemes tab active. In the Power Schemes drop-down list, you can select one of the preconfigured power schemes or you can create your own.

3. In the Power Schemes drop-down list, select Portable/Laptop.

4. In the Turn Off Monitor drop-down list, select After 10 Mins.

5. In the Turn Off Hard Disks drop-down list, select After 20 Mins.

6. Click Save As.

    The Save Scheme dialog box appears.

7. In the Save This Power Scheme As text box, type **Airplane** and then click OK.

8. Click the Apply button.

    Notice that Airplane appears in the Power Schemes drop-down list as the currently applied power scheme.

Note From now on, whenever you want to use the Airplane power scheme, you would select it here and then click the Apply button.

---

9. Click the Hibernate tab.

10. Select the Enable Hibernate Support check box, and then click the Apply button.

Note By selecting the Enable Hibernate Support check box and clicking the Apply button, you enable Hibernate mode on your computer.

---

11. Click the APM tab.

Note If you don't have an APM tab because your system doesn't have an APM-BIOS installed, skip this step and go to step 13.

---

12. Select the Enable Advanced Power Management Support check box, and then click the Apply button.

Note By selecting the Enable Advanced Power Management Support check box and clicking the Apply button, you enable APM support on your computer.

---

13. Click OK to close the Power Options Properties dialog box.

14. Close all open windows.

15. Log off your computer.

Lab 38: Using Device Manager and System Information

Objectives

After completing this lab, you will be able to

- Use Device Manager and System Information to monitor, review, and trouble-shoot your system configuration.

Estimated time to complete this lab: 15 minutes

Exercise 1
Using Device Manager to Review
Devices and to Troubleshoot a Device

In this exercise, you will use Device Manager to review the devices on your system and their status. You will also use Device Manager to simulate troubleshooting an unterminated Small Computer System Interface (SCSI) chain.

▶ **To use Device Manager**

1. Log on to the local computer as Administrator using a password of "password".

2. Right-click My Computer, and then click Manage.

   The Computer Management console opens.

3. In the console tree under System Tools, click Device Manager.

4. In the Details pane, double-click Disk Drives and then double-click one of the drives listed.

   The disk drive's Properties dialog box appears with the General tab active, showing a Device Status message box that indicates whether or not any problems exist with the drive.

5. Click the Troubleshooter button. (Normally you would only do this if Device Status indicated there was a problem.)

   Notice that Windows 2000 Help starts with Drives Troubleshooter displayed in the right pane. Troubleshooter steps you through a series of questions to help you resolve your problem.

6. On the What Problem Are You Having? page, select the I'm Having A Problem With My Hard Drive Or Floppy Disk Drive radio button and then click Next.

7. On the Are You Using A SCSI Device? page, ensure that the Yes, I'm Having A Problem With A SCSI Device radio button is selected and then click Next.

   On the Is The SCSI Chain Terminated? page, you are asked, "Does Your Device Work When You Terminate The SCSI Chain?" The system has suggested a possible resolution to your problem. You would have to determine if your SCSI chain was terminated. If the SCSI chain was not terminated, you would then terminate your SCSI chain and check to see whether or not your disk drive starting working.

   Notice there are three options:

   Yes, My Device Works.

   No, My Device Doesn't Work. Or The SCSI Chain Is Already Terminated.

   I Want To Skip This Step And Try Something Else.

For the purposes of this lab, you will assume that the SCSI chain was not terminated and that when you terminated it, the disk drive started working.

8. Click the Yes, My Device Works radio button, and then click Next.

   Assuming that an unterminated SCSI chain was the problem you were trying to solve, you would have just fixed the problem.

9. Close Windows 2000 Help and the disk drive's Properties dialog box.

Exercise 2
Using System Information

In this exercise, you will use System Information to view configuration information about your computer.

▶   **To use System Information**

1. Use the MMC to create a custom console, and add the System Information snap-in to the console, with the focus directed on the local computer.

2. On the Console 1 – [Console Root] console, double-click System Information in the console tree and then click System Summary.

   Notice that a Refreshing System Information message appears in the Details pane, while System Information takes a snapshot of the current system configuration.

3. Review the information displayed in the Details pane.

4. In the console tree, double-click Hardware Resources and then click IRQs.

   Look in the Details pane. Are there any IRQs being shared?

   _____

5. In the console tree, double-click Software Environment and then click Services.

6. In the Details pane, review which services are running and which services are stopped.

7. Save the custom console containing the System Information snap-in. On the Action menu, click Save As System Information File.

8. The Save As dialog box appears.

   Notice that by default the file is saved in the My Documents folder.

9. In the File Name text box, type **System Information** and click the Save button.

   It will take a minute to save the file.

10. Minimize the Console 1 custom MMC console.

11. Open the C:\Documents And Settings\Administrator\My Documents\System Information file.

   What did you save in the System Information file?

   _____

12. Close all windows.

Lab 39: Using the Windows Signature Verification Utility

Objectives

After completing this lab, you will be able to

- Use the Windows Signature Verification utility.

Estimated time to complete this lab: 10 minutes

Exercise 1
Using the Windows Signature Verification Utility

In this exercise, you will use the File Signature Verification utility (sigverif) to monitor and troubleshoot driver signing on your system.

▶ **To use sigverif**

1. Click the Start button, and then click Run.

   The Run dialog box appears.

2. In the Open text box, type **sigverif** and then press ENTER.

   The File Signature Verification dialog box appears.

3. Click the Advanced button.

   The Advanced File Signature Verification Settings dialog box appears with the Search tab active. Notice that by default, you are notified if any system files are not signed. Notice also that you can select the Look For Other Files That Are Not Digitally Signed radio button. When this option is selected, the File Signature Verification utility checks the nonsystem files to see whether or not they are digitally signed. If you select this option, you can specify the search parameters for the files you want checked.

4. Leave the default setting of Notify Me If Any System Files Are Not Signed selected, and then click the Logging tab.

   Notice that by default, the File Signature Verification utility saves the file signature verification to a log file, named Sigverif.txt.

5. Leave the default settings, and click OK to close the Advanced File Signature Verification Settings dialog box.

6. In the File Signature Verification dialog box, click the Start button.

   When the File Signature Verification utility completes its check, a Signature Verification Results window will appear if there are files that are not signed. Otherwise you will see a SigVerif message box telling you that your files have been scanned and verified as digitally signed.

7. If you get a Signature Verification Results window, review the results and then close the Signature Verification Results window. Otherwise, click OK to close the SigVerif message box.

8. Close the File Signature Verification utility.